THE WORLD FROM ABOVE

GET A BIRD'S-EYE VIEW OF THE PLANET

ACKNOWLEDGEMENTS
Author: Ben Hubbard
Publishing Director: Piers Pickard
Publisher: Rebecca Hunt
Editorial Director: Joe Fullman
Art Director: Andy Mansfield
Print Production: Nigel Longuet

Published in September 2025
by Lonely Planet Global Ltd

CRN: 554153
ISBN: 978-1-83758-624-0
www.lonelyplanet.com/kids
© Lonely Planet 2025

Printed in Malaysia
10 9 8 7 6 5 4 3 2 1

STAY IN TOUCH
lonelyplanet.com/contact

Lonely Planet Office:
IRELAND
Digital Depot, Roe Lane (off Thomas St),
Digital Hub, Dublin 8, D08 TCV4

MIX
Paper | Supporting responsible forestry
FSC™ C021741

Paper in this book is certified against the Forest Stewardship Council™ standards. FSC™ promotes environmentally responsible, socially beneficial and economically viable management of the world's forests.

Lonely planet KIDS

THE WORLD FROM ABOVE

BEN HUBBARD

CONTENTS

THE HIGH VIEW

Seeing views of the world from high above is something that's usually enjoyed only by birds, passengers in aeroplanes and astronauts. But today, modern satellite and drone images allow all of us to gaze down on our planet – while keeping our feet firmly on the floor. What do we see?

In this book, we'll find out as we tour the world, continent by continent, to zoom in (and out) on many of its most interesting parts. On the way, we'll get rare glimpses of some wonderful things: incredible landmarks, like the Statue of Liberty, the Giza Pyramids and the Great Wall of China; natural wonders such as Niagara Falls, the Amazon River and herds of wildebeest on the African plains; and extraordinary cities, including New York, London, Cape Town, Tokyo and Sydney.

Welcome to *The World from Above*!

CROP FIELDS, KANSAS, USA

You might think this is an image of an artwork. In fact, it shows circular fields of corn, each several hundred metres across. Located in a dry region, the fields are watered by central sprinklers which givea them their round shapes.

GRAND PRISMATIC SPRING, USA p.20

GOLDEN GATE BRIDGE, USA p.18

GRAND CANYON, USA p.22

NORTH AMERICA

Many of North America's key physical features are clearly visible from space. These include the icy regions of the north, the great lakes of the east, the dense forests of central America, the parched deserts of the southwest and various snow-capped mountain ranges. The continent's territory is dominated by the three giant countries of Canada, the United States and Mexico. But it also contains several smaller territories in central America and the islands of the Caribbean.

MEXICO CITY, MEXICO p.24

From above, you can see the whole of the White House, perhaps the most famous building in the USA. The central white building is where the president lives. On either side are offices, known as the West and East Wings, where officials work.

NIAGARA FALLS, CANADA–USA p.10

NEW YORK, USA p.12

CHICHEN ITZA, MEXICO p.26

PANAMA CANAL, PANAMA p.28

CN TOWER, TORONTO, CANADA

This was the world's tallest building from 1976 to 2007 when it was surpassed by the Burj Khalifa in Dubai, UAE. But, at 553.3 m (1,815 ft), this observation and communications tower still dominates Toronto's skyline.

GREAT BLUE HOLE, BELIZE

Measuring 300 m (984 ft) across and 125 m (410 ft) deep, the Great Blue Hole is a massive marine sinkhole off the coast of Belize. Note how small the ship anchored on it looks compared to the vast hole.

NIAGARA FALLS
CANADA–USA

WHAT?

One of North America's most visited natural wonders, Niagara Falls is a series of three waterfalls that lie on the Niagara River between Canada and the United States. Thousands of tonnes of water plunge over the falls every minute, making the roaring sound that gives Niagara its name – meaning 'thunder of water' in the local Iroquois language. Note how roads, restaurants and hotels now surround the falls, servicing the millions of tourists who flock here every year to watch from boats and viewing platforms.

WHERE?

On the US–Canada border between the province of Ontario, Canada, and the state of New York, USA

Sightseeing boats give tourists the chance to get close enough to the falls to experience a drenching without actually drowning. The open-air, electric boats transport passengers upriver, around the edge of the falls, and back to shore 10 minutes later. Waterproof ponchos are provided (and are very much required).

CLOSE-UP

DAM

HORSESHOE FALLS

BRIDAL VEIL FALLS

AMERICAN FALLS

Of the three waterfalls at Niagara, the biggest is the curved Horseshoe Falls (main picture), which lies right on the border of Canada and the USA. Measuring 792 m (2,600 ft) along its curve and 48 m (158 ft) high, it draws in around 90 per cent of the river's water. Beyond this are two smaller falls: Bridal Veil Falls and American Falls. A dam above the falls controls the flow of water to all.

STATUE OF LIBERTY p.14

STATEN ISLAND FERRY

The orange boat seen here approaching the skyscrapers of Downtown Manhattan is the Staten Island Ferry. Free to ride, the ferry transports 15 million passengers annually between Manhattan and Staten Island.

BROOKLYN BRIDGE

A wonder of 19th-century engineering, the Brooklyn Bridge spans 486 m (1,595 ft) across the East River to connect the New York boroughs of Manhattan and Brooklyn. It opened in 1883.

EMPIRE STATE BUILDING

Though now only New York's eighth tallest structure, the 381 m (1,250 ft) tall Empire State Building is still its most famous. It was completed in 1931.

NEW YORK CITY
USA

WHAT?

Here, we're gazing down on the USA's largest city, New York. The long strip of land in the centre is the island of Manhattan, the heart of the metropolis. Its two main clusters of skyscrapers represent the Downtown and Midtown areas. Near Midtown is the calm green space of Central Park, while to the right, across the Hudson River, is the state of New Jersey.

WHERE AND WHEN?

- In New York State, east coast of USA

- City founded in 1624

FIFTH AVENUE

A shopping street that runs past Central Park and for much of the length of Manhattan, Fifth Avenue is famed for its swanky stores. Its traffic lanes are often filled with the city's iconic yellow taxis.

CENTRAL PARK p.16

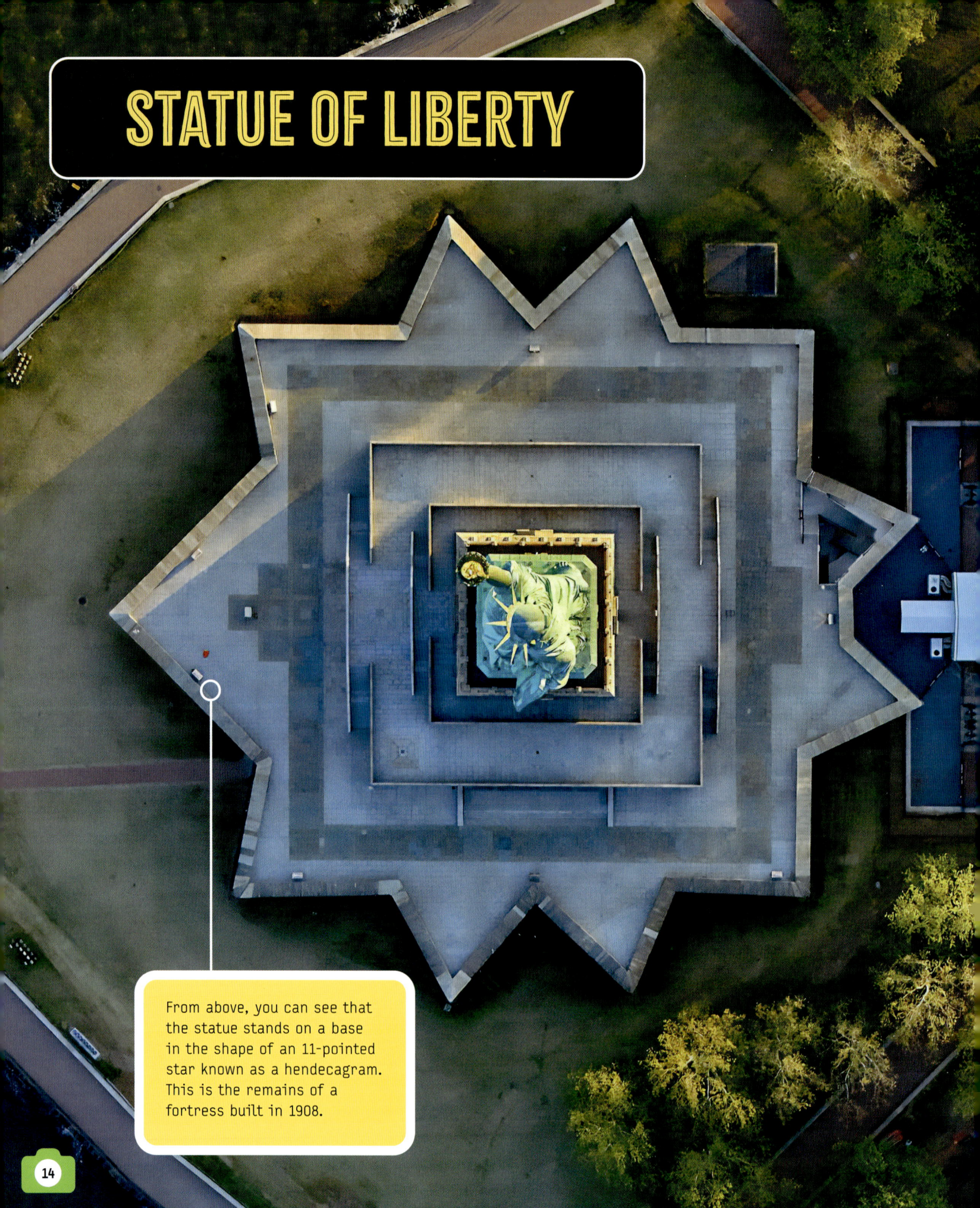

STATUE OF LIBERTY

From above, you can see that the statue stands on a base in the shape of an 11-pointed star known as a hendecagram. This is the remains of a fortress built in 1908.

WHERE AND WHEN?

- On Liberty Island, New York, USA
- Finished in France in 1884; reassembled in the USA in 1887

WHAT?

A symbol both of New York and the USA, the torch-carrying statue is 46 m (151 ft) high. Standing on New York's Liberty Island, just south of Manhattan, it was a gift from France to commemorate the American Revolution. In the following decades, it greeted millions of European immigrants arriving by ship to begin new lives in the United States of America.

CLOSE-UP

Originally built in France and shipped in crates to be reconstructed in America, the statue is made from 300 thin, copper sheets riveted together over an iron framework. Visitors can pre-book to climb the 354 interior steps to catch a view of New York City from the 25 windows in the statue's crown.

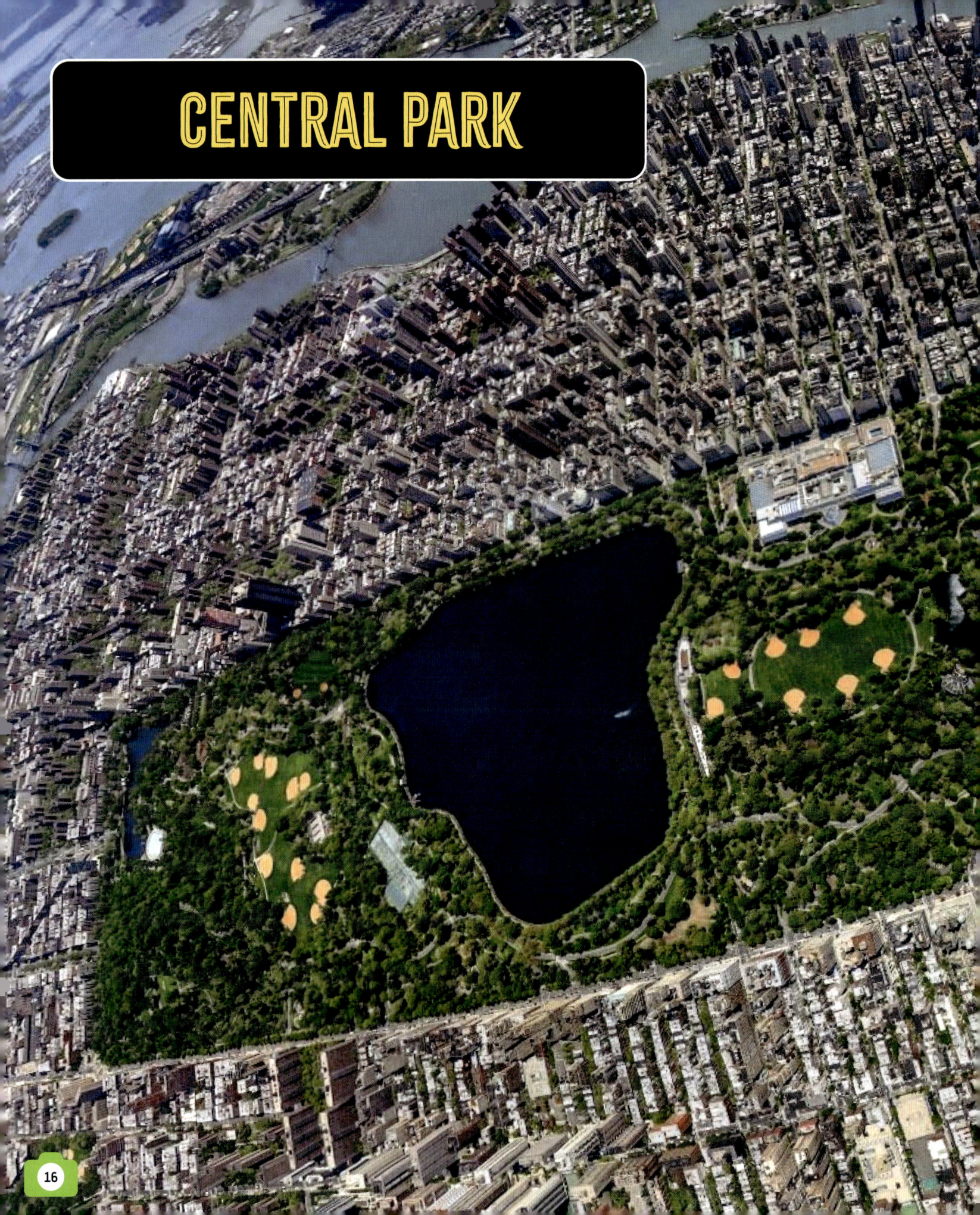

CENTRAL PARK

WHAT?

Known as the 'Lungs of the city', Central Park is a 430-hectare (840-acre) leafy-green rectangle in the heart of urban Manhattan. A marvel of design, the park took nearly 20 years to develop. Today, it contains fields, lawns, sculptures, fountains, playgrounds, ice-skating rinks and three lakes. The large white building in the park is The Metropolitan Museum of Art (or 'The Met').

WHERE AND WHEN?

• In the centre of Manhattan, New York, USA

• Park completed in 1776

GOLDEN GATE BRIDGE
SAN FRANCISCO, USA

This iconic, instantly recognisable American landmark is 227 m (745 ft) high and 1,280 m (4,200 ft) long, but just 27 m (90 ft) wide. From above (left), you can see that it has six lanes of traffic, three in each direction.

WHERE?

• On Golden Gate strait, linking San Francisco city with Marin County, California, USA

CLOSE-UP

The bridge's steel framework was welded together with over 1.2 million rivets. Workers wore goggles and masks to protect against the toxic fumes the red-hot rivets released from the lead-based paint. The bridge's reddish colour is officially known as 'International Orange'.

To build the longest and tallest suspension bridge attempted to that point, workers in the 1930s toiled for four years in freezing fog, howling gales and the powerful, churning tides of San Francisco Bay. Designed by chief engineer Joseph Strauss to bend, sway and flex in the wind, the two-towered, steel-cabled bridge was completed in 1937, despite several deaths and construction disasters.

WHEN?

GRAND PRISMATIC SPRING
YELLOWSTONE NATIONAL PARK, USA

A dazzling wonder of blues, yellows, greens and oranges, the Grand Prismatic Spring is Yellowstone's largest hot spring at 112.8 m (370 ft) in diameter. Visitors can view the attraction on nearby walkways – positioned at a safe distance, as the water at the spring's blue centre can reach a scalding 87°C (189°F).

WHAT?

The spring is one of the most recognisable features of Yellowstone, the world's first national park. Covering an area of 8,992 sq km (3,472 sq miles), the park contains mountains, forests and rivers, as well as erupting geysers and hot springs.

CLOSE-UP

The colours of the Grand Prismatic Spring are formed by microbes living in the hot water. Different microbes thrive at the different temperatures around the spring's edge, and produce different colours. Some yellow-producing microbes group together to form thick, round mats, shown here.

WHAT?

Around six million years ago, the Colorado River began carving a cavernous gorge through Arizona to create what we now know as the Grand Canyon. Today, the canyon is 446 km (277 miles) long, between 0.2 and 29 km (0.1–18 miles) wide, and more than 1.6 km (1 mile) deep in some places. The canyon's spectacular size, shape and colours make it a popular tourist hotspot.

WHERE AND WHEN?

• In Grand Canyon National Park, Arizona, USA

• Park opened in 1919

GRAND CANYON
USA

HORSESHOE BEND

Every year, more than two million tourists flock to the Grand Canyon's Horseshoe Bend, where the Colorado River has carved out a giant 270-degree curve. Visitors can view the rock formation and the bright blue and emerald-green river around it from a lookout 300 m (1,000 ft) above.

In this satellite image taken from space, we can see how the canyon follows the twists and turns of the Colorado River that created it. In total, the river flows for 2,330 km (1,447 miles) all the way down to Mexico. With help from wind and rain, the river has worn the soft sedimentary rocks of the canyon into a wonderland of valleys, cliffs and temple-like towers.

MEXICO CITY
MEXICO

ANGEL OF INDEPENDENCE

Erected in 1910 to commemorate Mexico's War of Independence, the Angel of Independence is one of Mexico City's best-loved landmarks. Built on a mausoleum for Mexican war heroes, the monument features a 36 m (118 ft) high column topped by a gold statue of the Greek goddess of victory, Nike.

PLAZA DE TOROS

The largest bull ring in the world, the plaza opened in 1946. It can seat over 40,000 people, though it was closed down for two years following legal challenges by animal rights' groups in 2022. The neighbouring structure is a small football stadium.

TAPO BUS TERMINAL

WHAT?

The largest metropolis in North America, Mexico City is home to over 22 million people. Ringed by mountains, which limit its room to expand, it's a densely packed place – as this image taken from high above shows. Founded in the 16th century, it was built directly over the city of Tenochtitlan, the capital of the Aztec Empire, following its conquest by Spanish invaders.

WHERE AND WHEN?

- In the Valley of Mexico, Central Mexican Plateau, Mexico
- City founded in 1524

PLAZA DEL EJECUTIVO

Situated in the city's Venustiano Carranza district, the Plaza Del Ejecutivo is a circular park with a spider-web shaped neighbourhood built around it. Home to around 440,000 people, the area's design was based on the Italian Renaissance town of Palmanova.

Commonly called TAPO, the circular, dome-covered Terminal de Autobuses de Pasajeros de Oriente transports over 10,000 bus passengers to 14 states across Mexico every day. Here you can see buses parked most of the way round the perimeter. The terminal was built in 1978 and also contains a central food court and a market that distributes free books.

Chichen Itza's ballcourt is one of the city's most interesting – and grisly – features. Players had to shoot a heavy rubber ball through hoops in the wall using any part of their body, except their hands and feet. The game may have ended with some of the players being sacrificed.

CHICHEN ITZA
MEXICO

WHAT?

The ruins of the Maya city of Chichen Itza are surrounded by forest. Laid out around a central step-pyramid temple, the city was at its peak in around 800 CE when it was home to some 35,000 people. Later, the city declined and was reclaimed by the jungle, but was uncovered in the 19th century.

WHERE AND WHEN?

- In south-central Yucatan State, Mexico
- City built from c. 600–750 CE

TZOMPANTLI (SKULL PLATFORM)

A large, rectangular stone platform, Chichen Itza's *Tzompantli* depicts racks of carved stone skulls threaded through vertical poles. Real skulls were once displayed on the platform in this way. It is believed players of the Maya ball game were beheaded and had a hole drilled through their skull, which was then attached to a long pole and added to the platform.

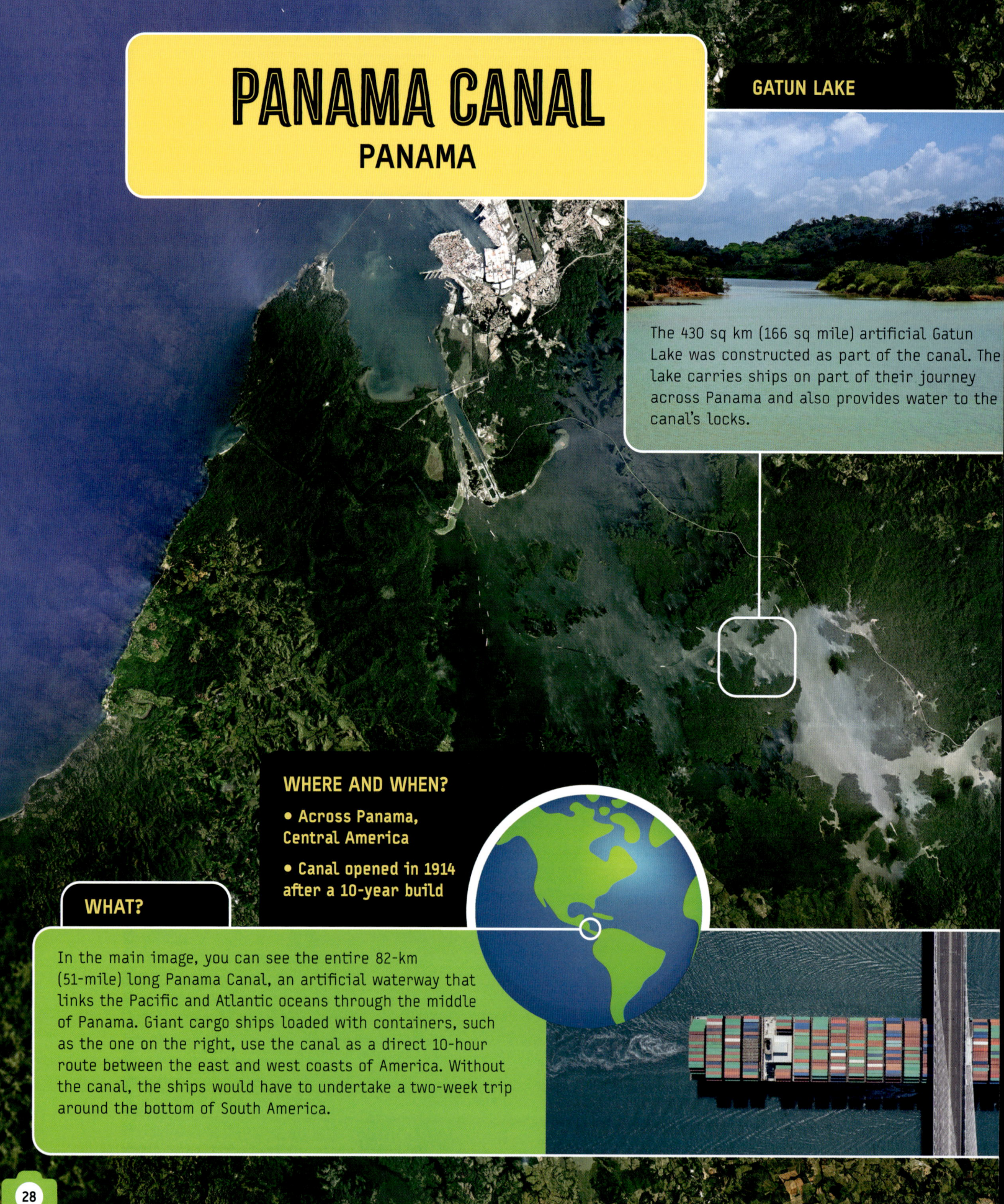

PANAMA CANAL
PANAMA

GATUN LAKE

The 430 sq km (166 sq mile) artificial Gatun Lake was constructed as part of the canal. The lake carries ships on part of their journey across Panama and also provides water to the canal's locks.

WHERE AND WHEN?

• Across Panama, Central America

• Canal opened in 1914 after a 10-year build

WHAT?

In the main image, you can see the entire 82-km (51-mile) long Panama Canal, an artificial waterway that links the Pacific and Atlantic oceans through the middle of Panama. Giant cargo ships loaded with containers, such as the one on the right, use the canal as a direct 10-hour route between the east and west coasts of America. Without the canal, the ships would have to undertake a two-week trip around the bottom of South America.

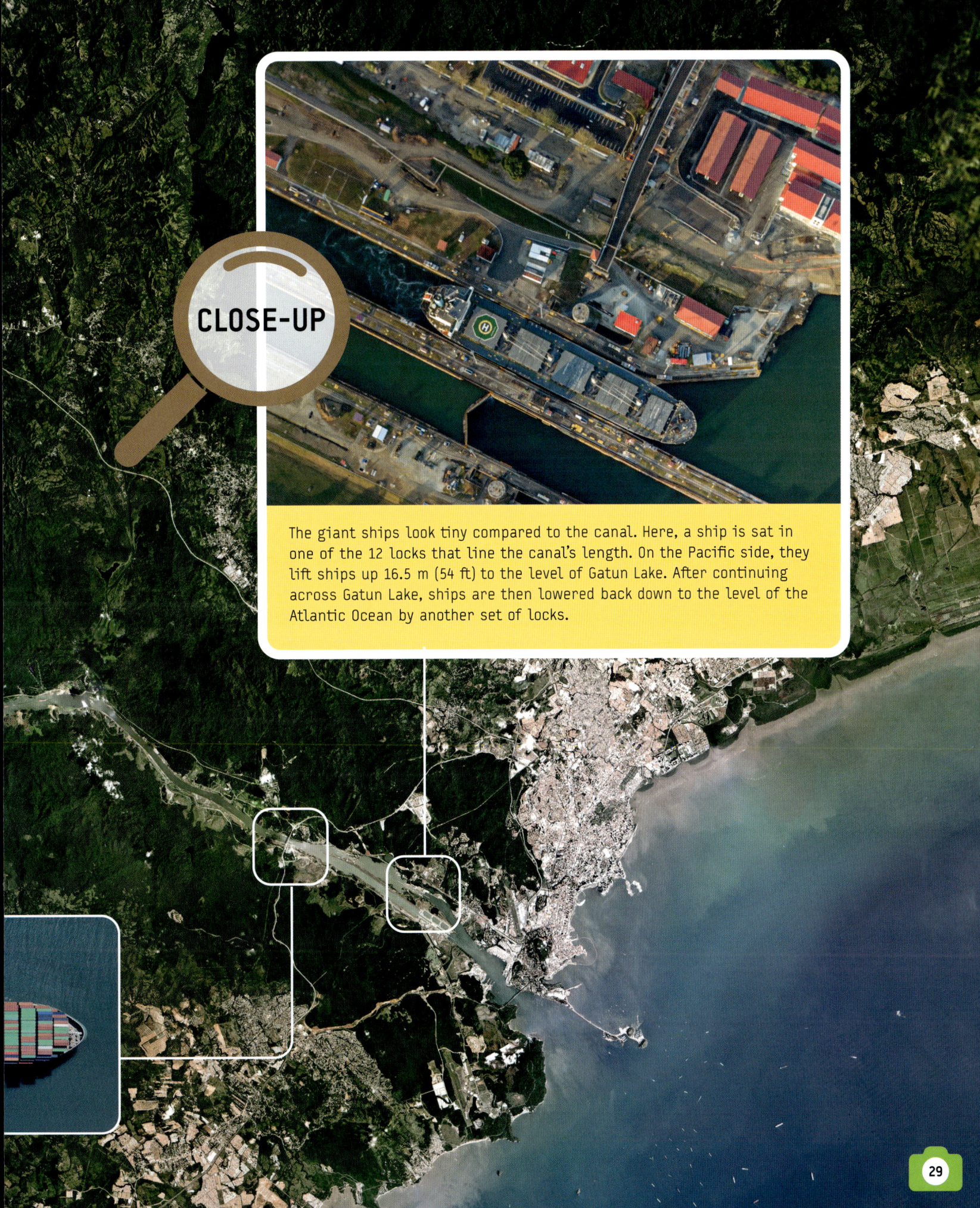

CLOSE-UP

The giant ships look tiny compared to the canal. Here, a ship is sat in one of the 12 locks that line the canal's length. On the Pacific side, they lift ships up 16.5 m (54 ft) to the level of Gatun Lake. After continuing across Gatun Lake, ships are then lowered back down to the level of the Atlantic Ocean by another set of locks.

SOUTH AMERICA

From space, it's easy to make out some of South America's amazing geography. Its northern half is a dense mass of green, marking the extent of the mighty Amazon, the world's largest rainforest. You can also see the bright white of the Salar de Uyuni, the planet's most extensive salt flat. The brown area snaking down the western edge of the continent is the Andes, the world's longest mountain range, its southern peaks touched by snow.

ANGEL FALLS, VENEZUELA p.32

NAZCA LINES, PERU

The Nazca Lines were designed to be seen from high above. They're a collection of giant images, such as this hummingbird, etched onto the desert floor. They were created between 200 BCE and 600 CE by the Nazca people for unknown reasons – perhaps as messages for the gods?

TATACOA DESERT, COLOMBIA

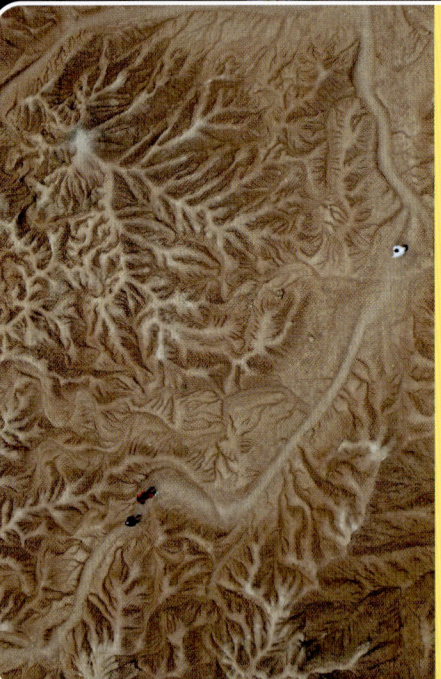

This may look like an image of mountains taken from high above, but peer closely and you'll see people, showing these peaks' true scale. They form part of Colombia's Tatacoa Desert.

JURUÁ RIVER, BRAZIL p.34

MACHU PICCHU, PERU p.36

SALAR DE UYUNI, BOLIVIA p.40

RIO DE JANEIRO, BRAZIL p.42

ATACAMA DESERT, CHILE p.40

LA PLATA, ARGENTINA p.46

LAS CARACOLES PASS, CHILE

Here, you can see lorries and cars making the slow journey backwards and forwards along the Los Caracoles Pass. Sometimes called the 'Snail's Pass', the road lies on the Chile-Argentina border and climbs to an oxygen-sapping 3,175 m (10,419 ft) above sea level.

EASTER ISLAND, CHILE

This is a small group of more than 900 giant stone statues erected by the people of Rapa Nui (Easter Island) between 1250 and 1500 CE. The island lies over 3,500 km (2,200 miles) from Chile.

BRÜGGEN GLACIER, CHILE p.48

ANGEL FALLS
VENEZUELA

WHAT?

WHERE?

On the Auyán-tepui mountain, feeding the Churun River, Canaima National Park, Bolivar State, southeastern Venezuela

Surrounded by dense jungle, the towering Angel Falls are best viewed from above or by boat, approaching along the Churun River. This is the world's tallest waterfall. At its top, a great ribbon of water gushes over the edge of the flat-topped Auyán-tepui mountain and plunges 979 m (3,212 ft) to the bottom.

JIMMIE ANGEL'S PLANE

Angel Falls became famous around the world when American explorer Jimmie Angel accidentally spotted them in 1933 from his plane (shown below exhibited at a Venezuelan airport). He returned to the falls in 1937, but his plane's wheels became stuck in the mud on Auyán-tepui mountain. Jimmie and his three associates had to abandon the plane and trek for 11 days down the mountain to reach civilization.

CLOSE-UP

As the water from the top of Angel Falls plummets to the bottom, it fans out into a 150-m (492-ft) wide curtain of water. The water then continues to rush down through a series of cascades, rapids and pools. Visitors can swim in some of these pools as they gaze up at the majestic falls above them, which are more than three Eiffel Towers high.

JURUÁ RIVER
BRAZIL

WHERE?

Flowing from east-central Peru to the Amazon River near Tamaniqua, Brazil

WHAT?

Winding its way like a long, squiggly worm through the Amazon Rainforest, the Juruá River has the most bends and meanders of any river in the world. At the end of its 32,283 km (20,060 mile) journey, the river joins up with the world's largest river, the vast Amazon, as shown in the above image.

The river flows slowly through the thick Amazon Rainforest, forming great bends that almost double back on themselves. In some places, these bends have joined up, changing the course of the river and leaving behind free-standing bodies of water known as oxbow lakes.

CLOSE-UP

Why does the Juruá River meander more than other rivers around the world? Scientists think it is due to the large amount of sediment that the river carries with it. This sediment causes the formation of 'point bars' – sandy beaches on the inside bends of the river, which encourage the bend to both lengthen and turn.

MACHU PICCHU
PERU

WHAT?

The agricultural terraces and stone buildings of the ancient Inca city of Machu Picchu are located high in the tropical mountain forests of the Andes. Built in the mid-15th century, the city was abandoned following an invasion by conquerors from Spain a century later. It remained unknown to the wider world until being discovered by American professor Hiram Bingham in 1911.

WHERE AND WHEN?

- In the Andes Mountains, around 2,430 m (7,950 ft) up
- Citadel built in the mid-1400s

INTIHUATANA

Standing at Machu Picchu's highest point is a great piece of granite cut from the mountain's bedrock. Carved into a shape that resembles a sun dial, the stone was called *Intihuatana* by its discoverers, which means 'place to tie up the sun' in the Inca Quechua language. It's believed it may have been used in rituals or for astronomy.

INCA TRAIL

Machu Picchu provides the climax of the Inca Trail, one of the world's best-known hiking routes. The trek takes four to five days and covers over 80 km (50 miles), heading past various Inca ruins, through cloud forests and up and down the region's peaks. Its highest point is the mountain pass, *Warmi Wañusqa* or 'Dead Woman's Pass', shown here, which lies 4,200 m (13,780 ft) above sea level.

ATACAMA DESERT
CHILE–PERU

WHAT?

Between the Pacific Ocean and the Andes Mountains, the Atacama Desert is a thin brown strip of land with a big reputation. This is one of the driest places on Earth, receiving only around 1 mm (0.04 in) of rainfall a year. Though few people live here, its vast empty spaces are home to some amazing structures and technologies.

SALAR DE UYUNI p.40

WHERE?

Mostly across northern Chile, with a small section of desert in southern Peru

SALAR DE ATACAMA

The rectangular objects glinting like mirrors in this image are actually pools where one of the world's most valuable substances is extracted: lithium. The waters of the Salar de Atacama salt flat contain high levels of the metal. This is pumped into the pools and then left to evaporate in the Sun leaving behind the lithium to be collected.

CHUQUICAMATA MINE

From above, the Chuquicamata copper mine looks like a swirling white and brown artwork. It is, in fact, the largest open-pit mine in the world, which was built to exploit the world's fourth-largest deposit of copper. Digging out large stores of the metal from the mine has created its hollowed-out landscape that reaches down 1,000 m (3,300 ft).

ALMA

Here, the desert floor is dotted with 12-m (40-ft) wide dishes, all pointing up towards the sky. Together, the 66 dishes (not all shown here) form a giant telescope. Known as the ALMA (Atacama Large Millimetre Array), it collects radio waves from stars and galaxies that can be converted into images. The vast structure enjoys perfect stargazing conditions. It's located in a very dry area, 5,000 m (16,500 ft) above sea level, far away from any light pollution. Once the Sun sets, the only light is provided by the Moon and stars.

WHAT?

The sparkling white areas shown here are salt. On the right is a section of the Salar de Uyuni, the world's largest salt flat, which covers 10,489 sq km (4,050 sq miles). On the left is Lake Coipasa, a super salty body of water fringed with crusts of the evaporated mineral. Both lie on the Altiplano, one of Earth's highest plateaus, which also boasts volcanoes (the dark brown areas).

WHERE?

On the Altiplano plateau, Daniel Campos Province, southwest Bolivia

LAKE COIPASA

Shallow Lake Coipasa is fed by the Lauca River, whose waters contain dark, volcanic sediment. This washed-up sediment is pictured here, next to the blue lake water and white salt deposits.

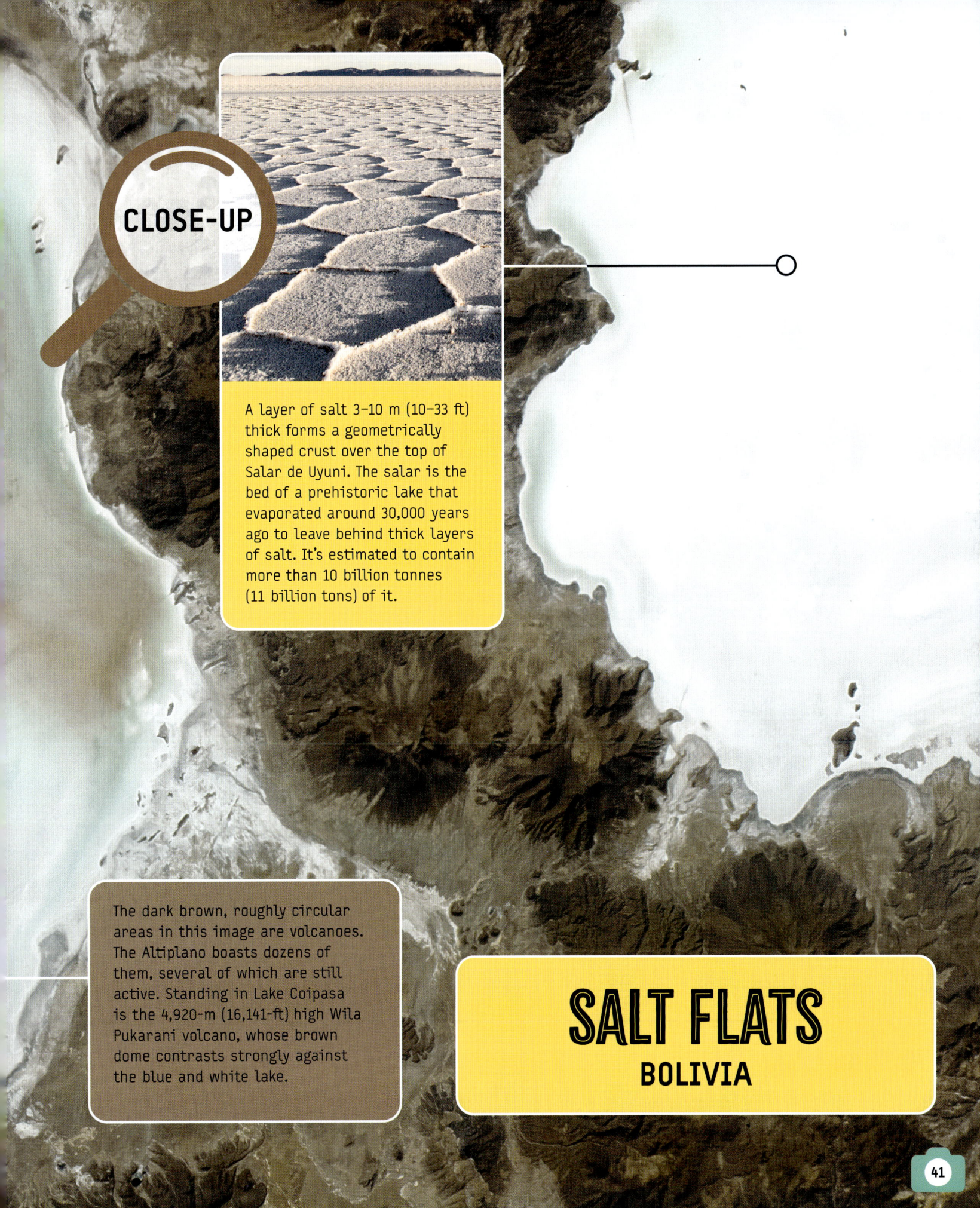

CLOSE-UP

A layer of salt 3–10 m (10–33 ft) thick forms a geometrically shaped crust over the top of Salar de Uyuni. The salar is the bed of a prehistoric lake that evaporated around 30,000 years ago to leave behind thick layers of salt. It's estimated to contain more than 10 billion tonnes (11 billion tons) of it.

The dark brown, roughly circular areas in this image are volcanoes. The Altiplano boasts dozens of them, several of which are still active. Standing in Lake Coipasa is the 4,920-m (16,141-ft) high Wila Pukarani volcano, whose brown dome contrasts strongly against the blue and white lake.

SALT FLATS
BOLIVIA

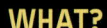

WHAT?

Rio de Janeiro is a spectacular, sprawling city built by a large natural bay. It was founded by the Portuguese in 1565, and is today famed for its carnivals, culture and samba dancing. Millions visit every year to enjoy the city's warm weather, colourful events and eye-catching landmarks – many of which can be picked out in this image.

WHERE?

Alongside Guanabara Bay on the Atlantic coast, southeast region, Brazil

MARACAÑA STADIUM

Opened in 1950, the Maracanã is Brazil's largest football stadium. At the 1950 World Cup final, it hosted the largest-ever crowd for a football game: 199,854 people. Today's seated capacity is 73,000.

COPACABANA BEACH

Here, we're looking directly down on the golden sand, colourful umbrellas and sunbathing bodies of a section of the Copacabana. This 4-km (2.5-mile) stretch of beach is one of Rio's most famous tourist spots, attracting thousands of sunworshippers and watersports enthusiasts every day.

CHRIST THE REDEEMER p.44

RIO DE JANEIRO
BRAZIL

RIO–NITEROI BRIDGE

This thin line stretching across the water is the continent's second-longest bridge. Completed in 1974, the 13.3-km (8.3-mile) long, 72-m (236-ft) high Rio–Niteroi Bridge spans Guanabara Bay and connects Rio de Janeiro to the neighbouring city of Niteroi.

SUGARLOAF MOUNTAIN

Sugarloaf Mountain is a cone-shaped peak at the entrance to Guanabara Bay. Named after the conical clay moulds that transported sugar aboard 16th-century ships, Sugarloaf mountain is 396 m (1,299 ft) high and can be enjoyed via a 1,400-m (4,600-ft) long cable car line that transports visitors to the top.

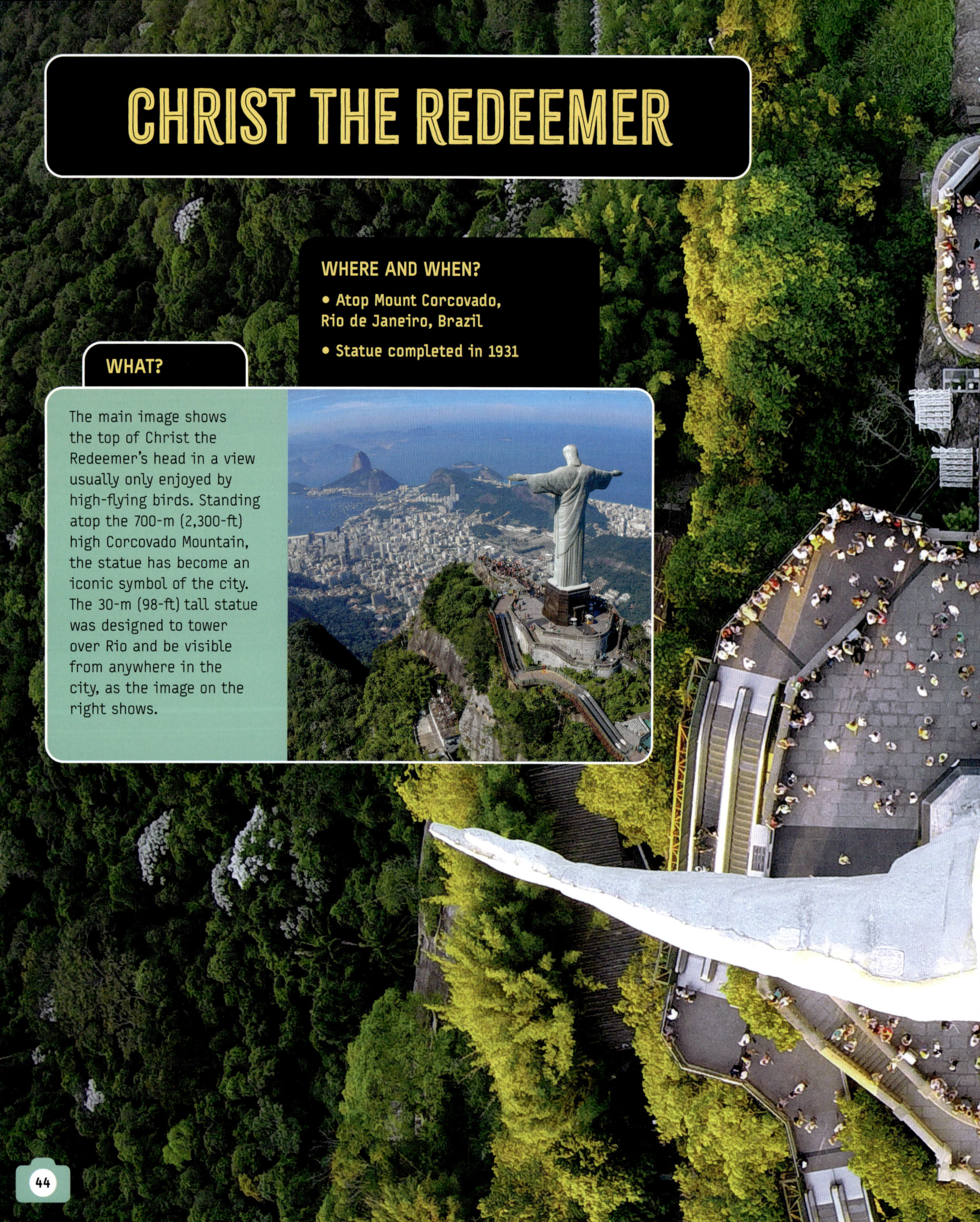

CHRIST THE REDEEMER

WHERE AND WHEN?

- Atop Mount Corcovado, Rio de Janeiro, Brazil

- Statue completed in 1931

WHAT?

The main image shows the top of Christ the Redeemer's head in a view usually only enjoyed by high-flying birds. Standing atop the 700-m (2,300-ft) high Corcovado Mountain, the statue has become an iconic symbol of the city. The 30-m (98-ft) tall statue was designed to tower over Rio and be visible from anywhere in the city, as the image on the right shows.

It looks solid but the statue is actually hollow. Made of reinforced concrete around a steel frame, and covered with thousands of small stone tiles, Christ the Redeemer contains staircases, platforms and passages. At the top are tunnels running through the statue's arms with hatches that open to let workers go outside.

LA PLATA
ARGENTINA

WHAT?

The unusual shape of La Plata city is best appreciated from high above. It's been laid out as a perfect square with four sides of equal length. Founded in 1882, its unique look was the brainchild of designer Pedro Benoit. He thought it would give the city a distinct identity to contrast it with neighbouring – and much more higgledy piggledy – Buenos Aires. Today, the city has a reputation as a centre of culture.

WHERE?

In Buenos Aires Province, 9 km (6 miles) inland from the Rio de Plata estuary, eastern Argentina

Right at the centre of La Plata is a large, square plaza which was designed to be at the heart of city life. Government buildings were constructed on the far side of the plaza while on this near side stands the Cathedral de La Plata. Though begun at the same time as the rest of the city, the cathedral wasn't completed until the 1990s, when its spires were finally added.

CLOSE-UP

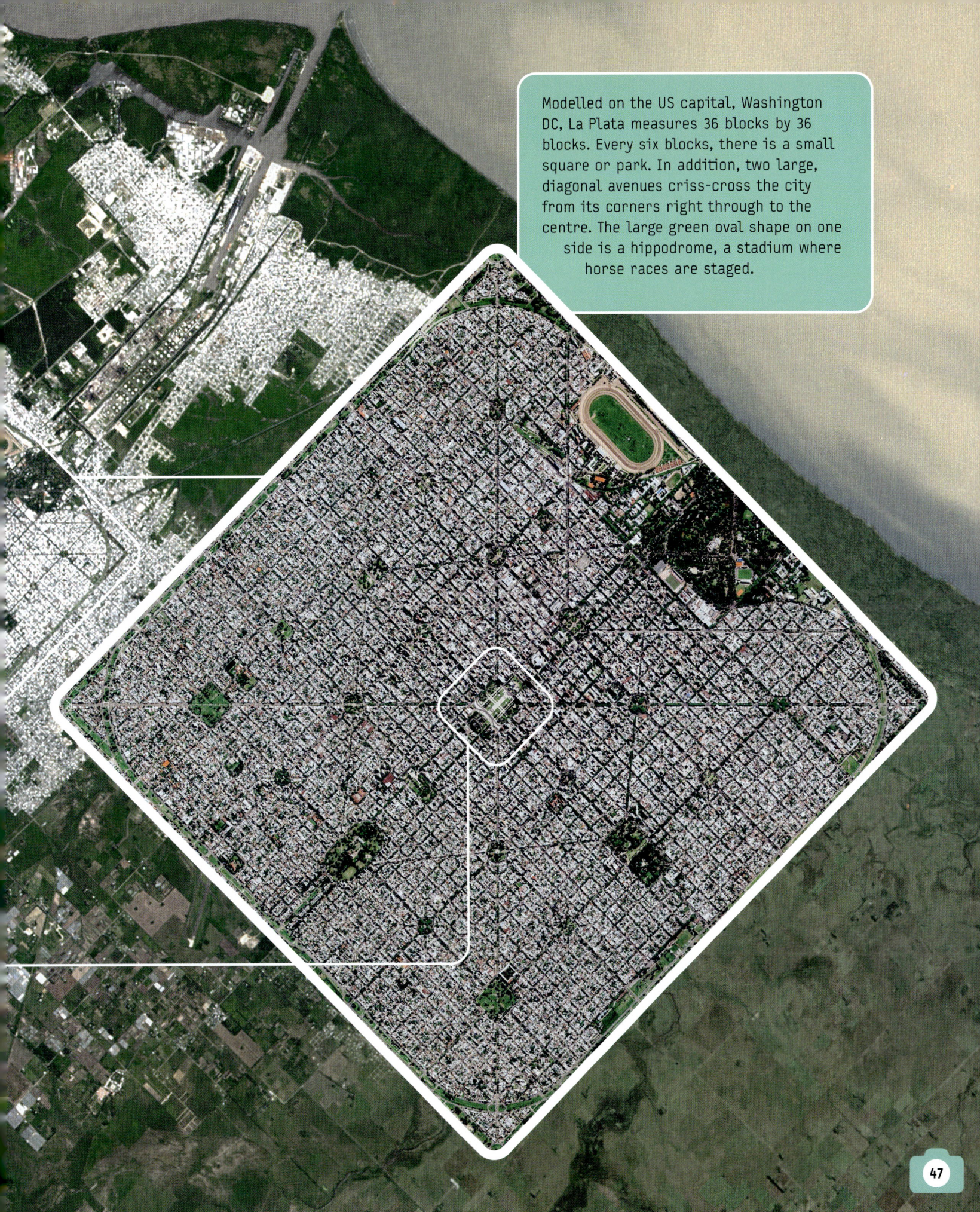

Modelled on the US capital, Washington DC, La Plata measures 36 blocks by 36 blocks. Every six blocks, there is a small square or park. In addition, two large, diagonal avenues criss-cross the city from its corners right through to the centre. The large green oval shape on one side is a hippodrome, a stadium where horse races are staged.

BRÜGGEN GLACIER
CHILE

CLOSE-UP

Seeing the Brüggen Glacier from above is a rare event. Clouds and storms usually cover Chile's Southern Patagonian Ice Field, shown in this main image. The glacier is one of several in the ice field. All were formed from compressed snow that built up during the last ice age over 12,000 years ago. Today, the Brüggen is the largest glacier in the Southern Hemisphere outside Antarctica.

WHERE?

In the Southern Patagonian Ice Field, southern Chile, near the southern end of South America

In this close-up image, we can see the end – or toe – of the Brüggen Glacier. That tiny white oblong just to the left is a cruise ship filled with tourists, who have come to gaze in wonder at the massive river of ice. And that ice is still growing. The glacier is one of the few across the world to have increased in size in the past century. From 1945 to 1976, it advanced around 10 km (6.2 miles), cutting off nearby Lake Greve from the sea. The lake is the light blue area just above and to the right of the glacier in the main image. Its colour is paler than the surrounding water due the presence of a milky sediment called 'glacier milk'. This is formed when glacial ice rubs against rock.

NEUSCHWANSTEIN CASTLE, GERMAN

This bird's-eye view shows the fairy-tale Neuschwanstein Castle perched on a forested outcrop of the Bavarian Alps. Its construction cost so much that the king who began it, Ludwig II, was deposed in 1886 for overspending. Its interior was never finished.

GEYSIR, ICELAND p.52

LONDON, UK p.54

GLASTONBURY FESTIVAL, UK p.56

PARIS, FRANCE p.58

EUROPE

Seen from hundreds of kilometres above Earth, Europe has a fertile-looking landscape of mostly greens and browns, reflecting its great stretches of countryside and forest. Several famous geographical features can be seen: the boot-like shape of Italy; the many islands of Greece; and the snowy-white of the Alps mountain range. Not visible at this scale are the continent's densely packed cities. For those, we'll need to zoom in a little closer...

SAGRADA FAMÍLIA, SPAIN p.66

ROME, ITALY p.64

THE ALPS p.60

PIRAEUS, ATHENS, GREECE

The main port of Athens, Piraeus was founded in the 5th century BCE – and has been much rebuilt since. It distinctive figure-eight shape is best viewed from above.

HENNINGSVÆR, NORWAY

A football pitch on a rocky island is an odd sight – especially for a community of only around 500. It was constructed for the people of the Henningsvær fishing village, which is spread over several small islands. Players have to be careful not to kick the ball into the sea.

ST BASIL'S CATHEDRAL, MOSCOW, RUSSIA

From the sky, the coloured domes of St Basil's Cathedral look like brightly packaged sweets in a chocolate box. Its construction was ordered by Tsar Ivan IV (better known as 'Ivan the Terrible') between 1555 and 1561.

GRAND CANAL, ITALY p.62

BOSPHORUS BRIDGE, ISTANBUL, TURKEY

Appearing dramatically out of the fog, this is one of the few bridges to link continents. It straddles the Bosphorus, a narrow stretch of water, separating the two halves of Istanbul, one of which sits in Europe and the other in Asia.

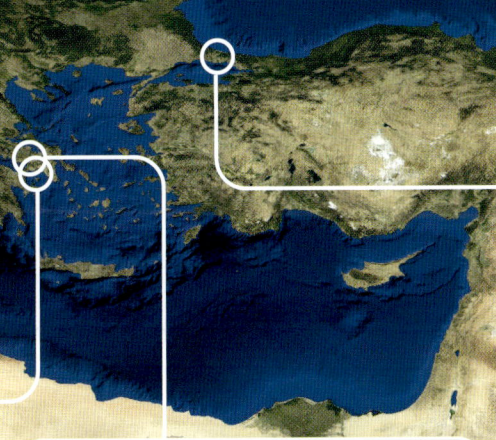

ACROPOLIS, GREECE p.68

GEYSIR GEOTHERMAL AREA
ICELAND

WHAT?

One of Iceland's top attractions, the Geysir Geothermal Area is a bubbling collection of hot springs, mud pools and erupting geysers. From above, the landscape is a mixture of reds, greens and yellows due to the presence of iron, copper and sulphur in the rocks. Paved pathways guide the many visiting tourists between the main sites.

WHERE?

In the Haukadalur Valley, east of the capital, Reykjavik, Iceland

STROKKUR

Strokkur is currently Iceland's most visited active geyser. Every six to ten minutes, it shoots a powerful jet of hot water 15 to 40 m (49 to 130 ft) up into the air, usually to the sound of applause from the amazed crowd looking on. The geyser was actually inactive for much of the 20th century. But it was reactivated in 1963 when local authorities cleared an underground inlet that had become blocked.

One of the other main sites in the area is Blesi: two hot springs that look a bit like a pair of spectacles from above. The striking blue colour of one of the pools – and of the Great Geysir – is caused by the element silica, which dissolves in the hot water. Although it looks inviting to soak in, the water of the Haukadalur Valley geysers seldom falls below a scalding-hot 40°C (104°F) – so bathers stay away!

THE GREAT GEYSIR

When seen from directly above, the Great Geysir looks like a deep-blue eye peering out from the landscape. This used to be Iceland's largest geyser, and would regularly fire a jet of boiling water up to heights of over 70 m (230 ft). However, it is now largely inactive and it can be years between eruptions. Nonetheless, this could still be regarded as the king of the geysers. After all, it's from where we get the English word 'geyser' – from the Icelandic for 'one that gushes'.

CLOSE-UP

BIG BEN

In this image, we can see one of the great icons of London – the clock tower Big Ben – towering over another: a red double-decker bus. Completed in 1859 (and officially known as the Elizabeth Tower), the 97.5-m (320-ft) high tower, stands next to the Houses of Parliament, home of the UK's government.

LONDON
ENGLAND, UK

LONDON EYE

Standing on the South Bank of the River Thames, the London Eye is a large observation wheel and one of London's most popular tourist attractions. Paying visitors can catch breath-taking views of the capital as they rotate 360 degrees to a height of 135 m (443 ft) above it.

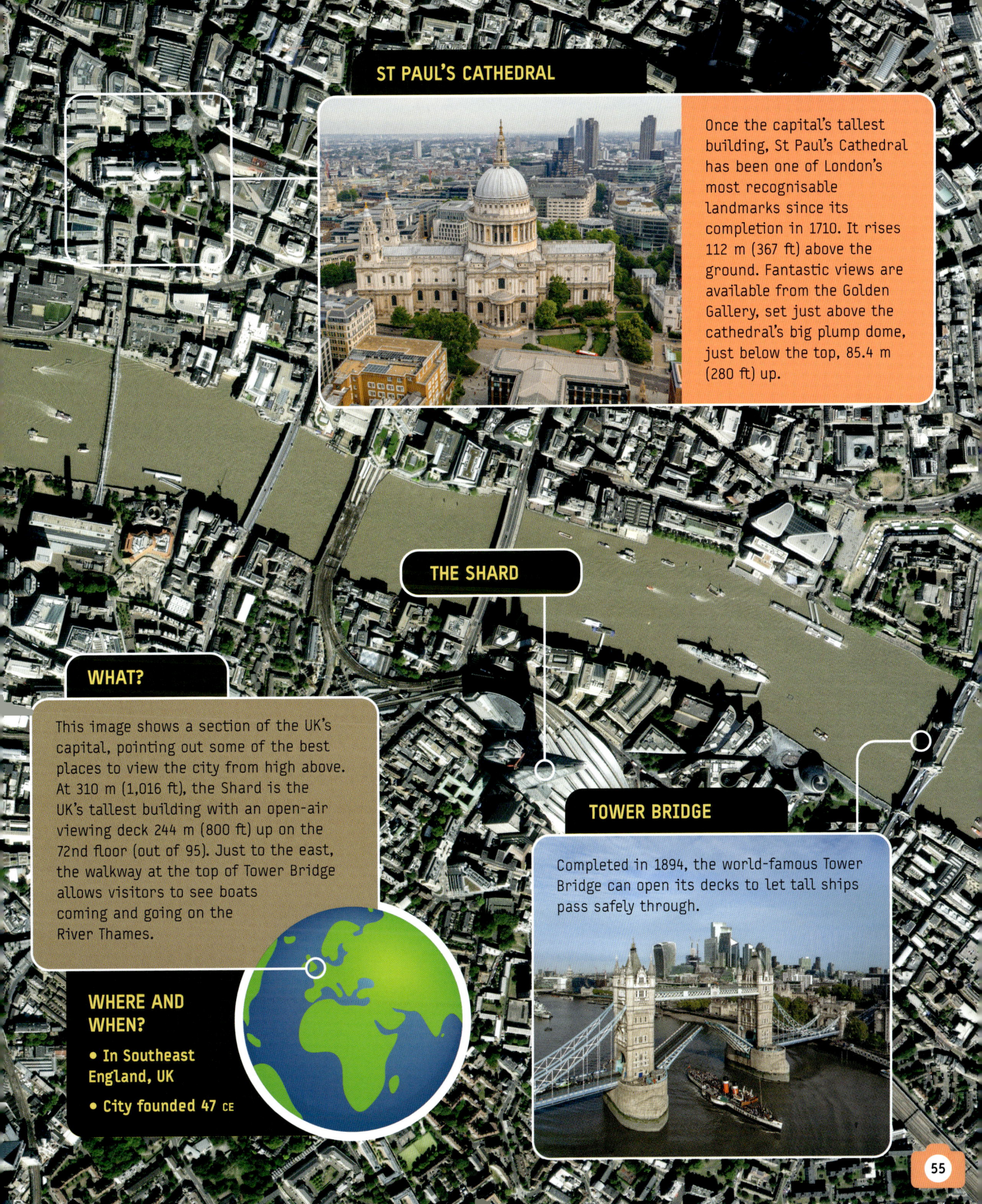

ST PAUL'S CATHEDRAL

Once the capital's tallest building, St Paul's Cathedral has been one of London's most recognisable landmarks since its completion in 1710. It rises 112 m (367 ft) above the ground. Fantastic views are available from the Golden Gallery, set just above the cathedral's big plump dome, just below the top, 85.4 m (280 ft) up.

THE SHARD

WHAT?

This image shows a section of the UK's capital, pointing out some of the best places to view the city from high above. At 310 m (1,016 ft), the Shard is the UK's tallest building with an open-air viewing deck 244 m (800 ft) up on the 72nd floor (out of 95). Just to the east, the walkway at the top of Tower Bridge allows visitors to see boats coming and going on the River Thames.

TOWER BRIDGE

Completed in 1894, the world-famous Tower Bridge can open its decks to let tall ships pass safely through.

WHERE AND WHEN?

• In Southeast England, UK

• City founded 47 CE

Glastonbury's largest and most famous venue is its Pyramid Stage. First constructed in 1971 from metal scaffolding and plastic sheeting, it's now a high-tech affair with screens either side showing close-ups of the performers. Up to 120,00 festival-goers can gather in front to watch the acts, which have included David Bowie, Bruce Springsteen and Stormzy.

GLASTONBURY FESTIVAL
ENGLAND, UK

The main image shows many of the tents, stalls and vehicles – not to mention some of the 200,000 music fans – that gather every year for Glastonbury, one of the world's largest outdoor festivals. First held in 1970, Glastonbury features top musical acts appearing across multiple stages.

WHERE AND WHEN?
- On Worthy Farm in Pilton, Somerset, England, UK
- Held most years since 1970, in June

CLOSE-UP

Here we can see a dense mass of tents. During the festival, the site becomes a giant camping ground with hundreds of portable toilets, catering vans and food stalls, and many performance tents and stages. Weather at Glastonbury is notoriously unpredictable, with heavy rains and flash floods at times washing out campsites and making the entire event a riotously muddy affair.

PARIS
FRANCE

ARC DE TRIOMPHE

Twelve avenues radiate out from the Place Charles de Gaulle, forming a star shape. At its centre is the 50-m (164-ft) high Arc de Triomphe, which was built in the early 19th century to commemorate those who had died fighting for France. It's 284 steps to the top from where there are great views.

EIFFEL TOWER

Here, we're peering down on one of the world's most famous landmarks: the Eiffel Tower. Standing 330 m (1,083 ft) high, the iron tower has three levels. Views from the third are 276 m (906 ft) above the ground.

THE LOUVRE

PLACE DE LA CONCORDE

Paris' largest public square is now a serene, beautiful place. At its centre stands a 3,300-year-old obelisk given to France by Egypt in 1829. In the late 18th century, however, during the French Revolution, this spot was occupied by a guillotine where dozens of people, including the king Louis XVI, were executed.

WHAT?

This satellite view shows Paris' neat parks and wide boulevards, as well as the many bridges spanning the River Seine that runs through the city's centre. France's capital is famed for its arts, architecture and cuisine. Every year, over 50 million tourists visit its landmarks, including the Louvre, the world's largest museum.

WHERE AND WHEN?
- In north-central France
- City founded 3rd century BCE

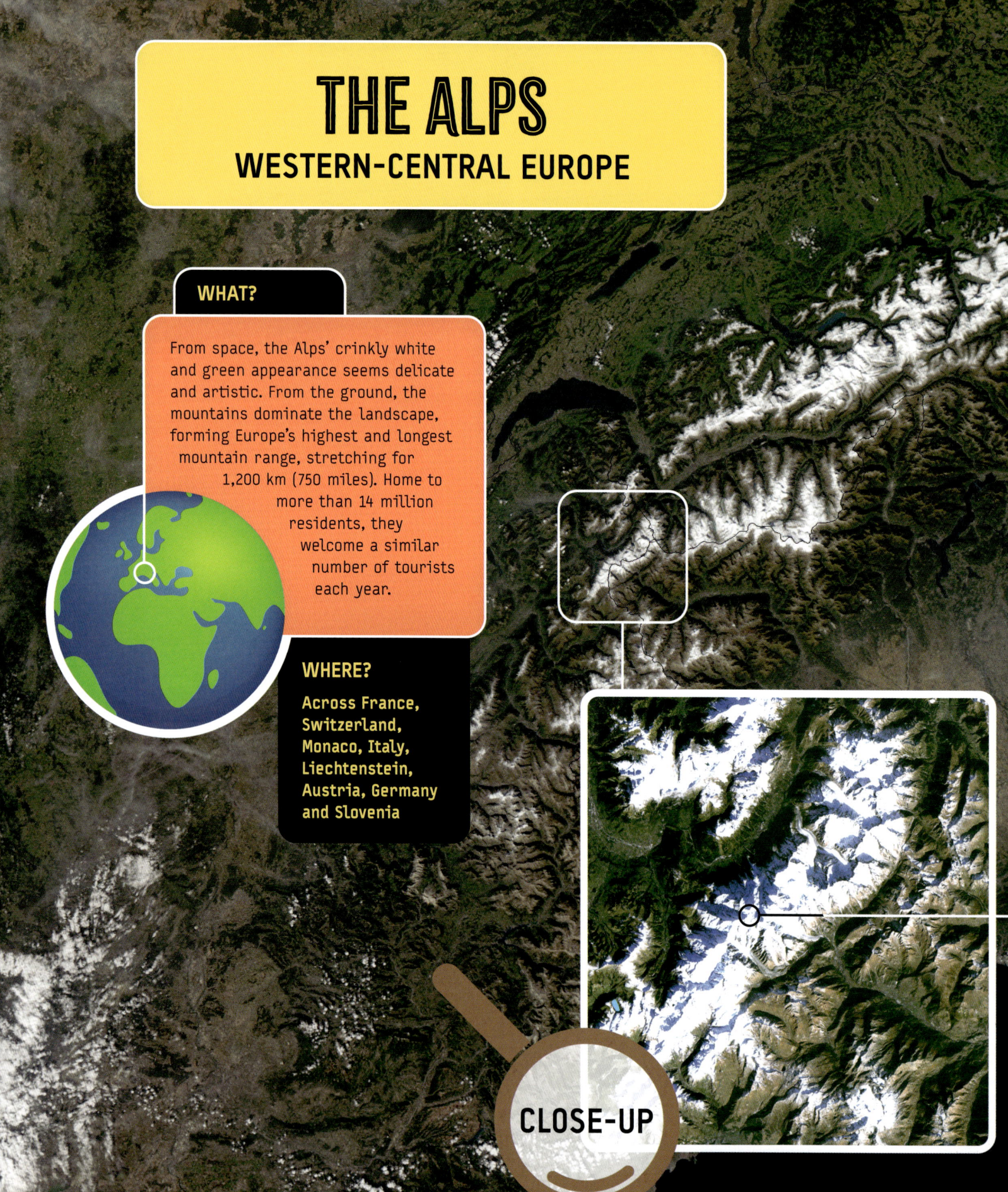

THE ALPS
WESTERN-CENTRAL EUROPE

WHAT?

From space, the Alps' crinkly white and green appearance seems delicate and artistic. From the ground, the mountains dominate the landscape, forming Europe's highest and longest mountain range, stretching for 1,200 km (750 miles). Home to more than 14 million residents, they welcome a similar number of tourists each year.

WHERE?

Across France, Switzerland, Monaco, Italy, Liechtenstein, Austria, Germany and Slovenia

CLOSE-UP

LANDWASSER VIADUCT

Despite the difficulty of the terrain, the Alps are criss-crossed by a network of railway lines. This image shows a train emerging from a tunnel and over a scenic viaduct in Switzerland. It's travelling on a line linking low-lying villages with the ski resort of St Moritz at 1,774 m (5,820 ft).

MONT BLANC

We have to zoom right in to pick out Western Europe's tallest mountain: Mont Blanc. Just a dot from far away, but a giant up-close, the mountain stands at 4,807 m (15,771 ft) on the French–Italian border. The glaciers and snow on its peak give it its name, meaning 'White Mountain'.

GRAND CANAL
VENICE, ITALY

CLOSE-UP

ST MARK'S SQUARE

The city's main open space, St Mark's Square is a paved open area filled with cafés, tourists and giant flocks of pigeons. Overlooking it are the magnificent St Mark's Clocktower, St Mark's Basilica (with its five domes) and the white horseshoe-shaped Doge's Palace where the city's medieval ruler used to reside.

Here we can see how Venice's 3-km (2-mile) long Grand Canal acts as the city's main thoroughfare. Instead of cars and buses, there are boats, barges and water taxis to transport people and goods around. Lining either side of the canal are churches, palaces, hotels and entrances to the smaller canals that act as the city's roads.

WHERE AND WHEN?

• In Venice, Veneto region, northeastern Italy

• City founded 5th century CE

RIALTO BRIDGE

This beautiful stone arch bridge was completed in 1591 and, for many years, was the only way people had of crossing the Grand Canal on foot. Then, as now, most journeys were taken by boat, including in the city's iconic black gondolas, several of which can be seen in this image. Today, the Rialto is one of four bridges on the Grand Canal out of a total of 472 across the whole city.

WHERE AND WHEN?
- In Lazio, Central Italy
- c. 8th century BCE

WHAT?

Originally built on seven hills, the Italian capital was once the centre of the most powerful civilisation in the world: the Roman Empire. Today, Rome's ancient ruins are still a big draw for the 35 million tourists that visit annually.

THE COLOSSEUM

Though nearly 2,000 years old, much of the largest amphitheatre of the Roman world is still standing. Up to 50,000 spectators once filled the seats that ran right round the central area. Here they could watch bloodthirsty entertainments, such as gladiator fights, bouts between humans and animals, mock naval battles and public executions.

ST PETER'S BASILICA

Contained within Rome is the Vatican City, home to the Pope, the head of the Catholic Church. At its centre is St Peter's Basilica (seen above on the left), a vast church built between 1506 and 1626, which still holds the record for the world's largest church interior. It stands next to St Peter's Square where up to 80,000 people regularly gather to hear the Pope speak.

CASTEL SANT'ANGELO

The star-shaped fortifications and gardens of the Castel Sant'Angelo can only be seen clearly from above. Once Rome's tallest building, the fortress was built in the mid-2nd century CE as a tomb for the Emperor Hadrian. In the Middle Ages, it was remodelled as a castle to protect the city's popes in times of danger.

ROME
ITALY

SAGRADA FAMÍLIA
BARCELONA, SPAIN

WHAT?

From above, the church of Sagrada Família stands clearly apart from the city's rectangular red roofs. Designed by Spanish architect Antoni Gaudi, the building's construction began in the late 19th-century. It was only a quarter complete in 1926 when Gaudi was struck by a tram and killed. Building work on the church is still continuing today.

WHERE AND WHEN?

• In Barcelona, Catalonia, Spain
• Church begun in 1882

This bird's-eye view shows the Sagrada Família's tall, twisting spires towering above Barcelona's buildings. And soaring above those is one of the cranes that are a near constant presence as building work continues. The church has been paid for entirely by donations, with the total cost of its 130-year construction estimated at US$389 million – and counting. When finally finished, Sagrada Família will be the tallest church in the world at 172.5 m (566 ft) and will have space for 13,000 worshippers.

ACROPOLIS
ATHENS, GREECE

CLOSE-UP

THE PARTHENON

Dominating the Acropolis is the Parthenon, a huge temple, some 70 m (228 ft) long and 19 m (62 ft) high. Its construction was ordered in the mid-5th century BCE by the great Athenian general Pericles to celebrate a military victory. Inside stood a 12-m (39-ft) high gold-and-ivory statue of Athena, the city's patron goddess. Though that has long vanished, much of the rest of the building remains.

From above, you can see how the ancient hilltop citadel known as the Acropolis is now surrounded by modern buildings. First built as a fortress on a rocky outcrop around 2500 BCE, it was later expanded into a white-marble city, containing public buildings, temples and a theatre. The term *acropolis* means 'high city' in ancient Greek.

WHERE AND WHEN?

• In Athens, Attica region, Greece

• Parthenon completed in 438 BCE

This lower-angle view shows how the Acropolis still dominates Athens' skyline, and how well preserved many of its buildings are. In addition to the Parthenon, sightseers can also visit a number of other smaller temples as well as an open-air theatre, shown in the bottom left of this picture. Known as the Odeon of Herodes Atticus, it was built in 174 CE and has rows of seating where audiences could watch plays performed on a semi-circular stage.

SAHARA DESERT, MOROCCO

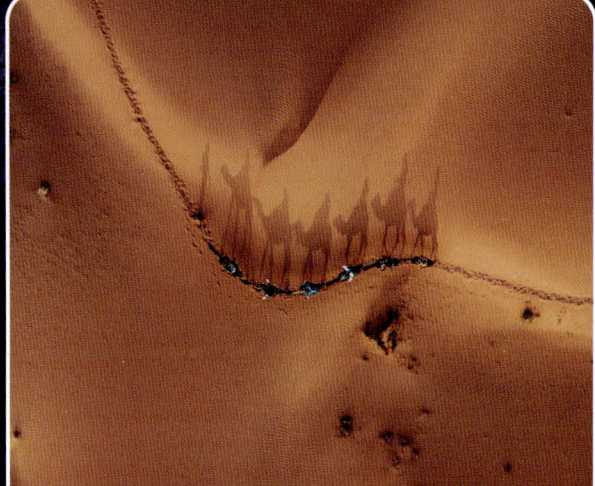

Here, the angle of the Sun has cast long shadows on the sand. This has created enormous images of a line of camels taking tourists on trip through Morocco's stretch of the Sahara Desert.

OUARZAZATE POWER PLANT, MOROCCO

One of the world's largest solar power stations, this is made up of thousands of mirrors. These focus and harness the hot desert Sun and turn it into electricity.

DJENNE, MALI p.74

MAKAKO, NIGERIA p.82

AFRICA

This satellite image shows Africa as a continent of extreme landscapes. The light, sandy colour taking up much of the north represents the world's largest hot desert, the vast Sahara. In the centre, a great swathe of green marks a more fertile region. The darkest patch is Earth's second-largest rainforest, the Congo. Enormous lakes stand out vibrantly in blue, while grasslands, shown in darker brown, occupy much of the east and south of the country.

SKELETON COAST, NAMIBIA

A shipwreck lies tossed onto the sand on one of the harshest coastlines on Earth. It's known as the Skeleton Coast because of the ship remains that litter the shore.

CAPE TOWN, SOUTH AFRICA p.90

GIZA PYRAMIDS, EGYPT p.72

FORT JESUS, MOMBASA, KENYA

Built for the king of Portugal and Spain in the late 16th century, this looks like a fairly standard – if imposing – fortress when viewed from the ground. But fly up into the air to view it as a bird would, and you can see that it was built in the shape of a man.

DALLOL HYDROTHERMAL SYSTEM, ETHIOPIA p.76

EL SOD, ETHIOPIA p.78

LUUQ, SOMALIA p.80

LE MORNE BRABANT, MAURITIUS

MARA RIVER, MASAI MARA, KENYA p.84

FISH RIVER CANYON, NAMIBIA p.88

Off the very southern tip of Mauritius, it looks like there's something impossible – an underwater waterfall. Water appears to cascade downwards, plummeting towards the seafloor. It's actually an optical illusion created by underwater currents and shifting sand patterns.

VICTORIA FALLS, ZAMBIA–ZIMBABWE p.86

GIZA PYRAMIDS
CAIRO, EGYPT

CLOSE-UP

All three pyramids were originally covered with a layer of smooth limestone blocks that would have made them dazzle in the Sun. Today, only Khafre's pyramid still has some of this layer left at its top, as shown on the left. If we zoom in to the top of the pyramid, we can see some of the 2-million plus stone blocks used to construct it. Each block weighs between 2.5 and 15 tonnes (3 and 16.5 tons).

WHAT?

On this page, we get a bird's-eye view of the pyramids of Giza. The three largest ones were constructed by the ancient Egyptians as tombs for their pharaohs around 4,500 years ago. The top one was built for Menkaure, the middle one for Khafre and the bottom one for Khufu. Khufu's pyramid, also known as the Great Pyramid, is the largest at 147 m (481 ft) tall. The smaller pyramids were where ancient Egyptian queens were buried.

WHERE AND WHEN?

• On the west bank of the River Nile, Cairo, Egypt

• Built between c. 2600 and 2500 BCE

DJENNE

MALI

WHAT?

From high above, the ancient city of Djenne looks like a series of lines and squares carved into wet clay. In a way, this is not too far from the truth – almost all of the buildings in Djenne's old town are constructed from sun-baked mud-bricks. This includes the Great Mosque, one of the continent's most famous buildings, which sits proudly in the centre of the city.

WHERE AND WHEN?

- On the banks of the River Bani, Mali

- City built c. 800 CE

Here we can see people carrying baskets of mud-plaster on their heads to the Great Mosque. Every year, the building's walls are re-plastered to help protect it against erosion and flooding.

This image shows a close-up of the mud-bricks used to construct Djenne's buildings. The bricks are made from river mud mixed with sand and clay, and placed into rectangular moulds. These are then left in the Sun to dry and harden before being used. The buildings are finally covered with mud-plaster to provide a smooth, protective finish.

CLOSE-UP

THE GREAT MOSQUE

Standing 16 m (52 ft) high, the Great Mosque is the largest mud-brick structure in the world. Its minarets tower above Djenne's other buildings. At the top of each sits an ostrich egg, a Mali symbol of fertility. Wooden beams protruding from the mosque's walls support the structure. They also act as scaffolding during the yearly re-plastering of the mosque. The mosque has been rebuilt three times since its original construction in the 13th century CE. This latest version dates back to 1907.

DALLOL HYDROTHERMAL SYSTEM
ETHIOPIA

WHAT?

The bright colours and swirling patterns make this area in Ethiopia seem like something from outer space. It's actually a hydrothermal field located next to the country's most active volcano, Erta Ale. The colours are caused by chemicals in the volcano's super-heated water.

WHERE AND WHEN?

• In the Danakil Depression, Erta Ale, Ethiopia

• Formed between 5 and 23 million years ago

The colourful Dallol Hydrothermal System covers an area of just 1 sq km (0.4 sq miles). If we zoom out, we can see it forms a small bright patch next to the dark brown in the centre of the volcano. The field is not just famed for its colours. The chemicals that form them also release pungent gases, which smell like rotten eggs due to the high levels of sulphur.

WHAT?

From space, El Sod looks like an ominous black hole in the ground. But by zooming in, it becomes clear that this is a large crater in a volcano with a lake at its centre. The lake's water is actually coloured blue. Luckily for visitors, the volcano is extinct.

WHERE?

Around 90 km (55 miles) from the town of Yabelo, southern Ethiopia

The lake is extremely salty and has thick deposits of salt around its edge – in fact, *El Sod* means 'The House of Salt' in the local language. While the water partially evaporates during summer, people extract the emerging salt, as shown in this picture. The salt is then crushed, dried in the Sun and sold to use in cooking.

CLOSE-UP

LUUQ
SOMALIA

SOMALIA

LUUQ

DRY RIVERBED

From the air, Somalia looks like a jagged piece of rock. Around 80 per cent of the country has an arid climate, and around a quarter is classified as desert. Water here is a precious commodity not to be wasted.

The city of Luuq has been built within a horseshoe-shaped bend of the River Jubba, one of the few sources of water in this dry land. Crop fields have been planted along the river's banks showing up as bright patches of green.

WHERE AND WHEN?

• In Gedo Province, Southwest Somalia

• City founded c. 15th century CE

DRY RIVERBEDS

Many of Somalia's waterways regularly dry out when conditions become too hot. This image shows some of these now water-free river valleys snaking across the landscape down to the coast on the Indian Ocean. To the right, winds have whipped the land into large, tan-coloured sand dunes.

MAKOKO
LAGOS, NIGERIA

WHAT?

WHERE AND WHEN?
- Next to the Third Mainland Bridge, on the coast of Lagos, Nigeria
- Established in the early 19th century

From above, Makoko looks like a city that's been flooded with water after a storm. In fact, it's a floating village that lies in the coastal waters of Nigeria. Established by fisher-people from Benin, Togo and Ghana, many of the Makoko homes have been built on long stilts to prevent the tidal seawater washing them away.

CLOSE-UP

Canoes are the main form of transport in Makoko, which, like Italy's Venice (see p.62), has a series of waterways instead of roads. The canoes are also used to fish for a large variety of seafood, which is both sold at markets and eaten fresh by the local community. It's estimated that around 100,000 people live here.

MARA RIVER, MASAI MARA
TANZANIA–KENYA

CLOSE-UP

This bird's-eye view looks like a column of ants on carefully clipped grass. In fact, it is a massive army of wildebeest, zebra and other animals on a months-long migration across a vast grassland, known as the Serengeti in Tanzania and the Masai Mara in neighbouring Kenya. Each animal that makes the journey successfully will have covered up to 1,000 km (600 miles).

Crossing the Mara River is among the migration's most dangerous moments. Here, crocodiles lurk in the shallows to bring down young, old, weak and sick animals. Thousands of wildebeest are caught.

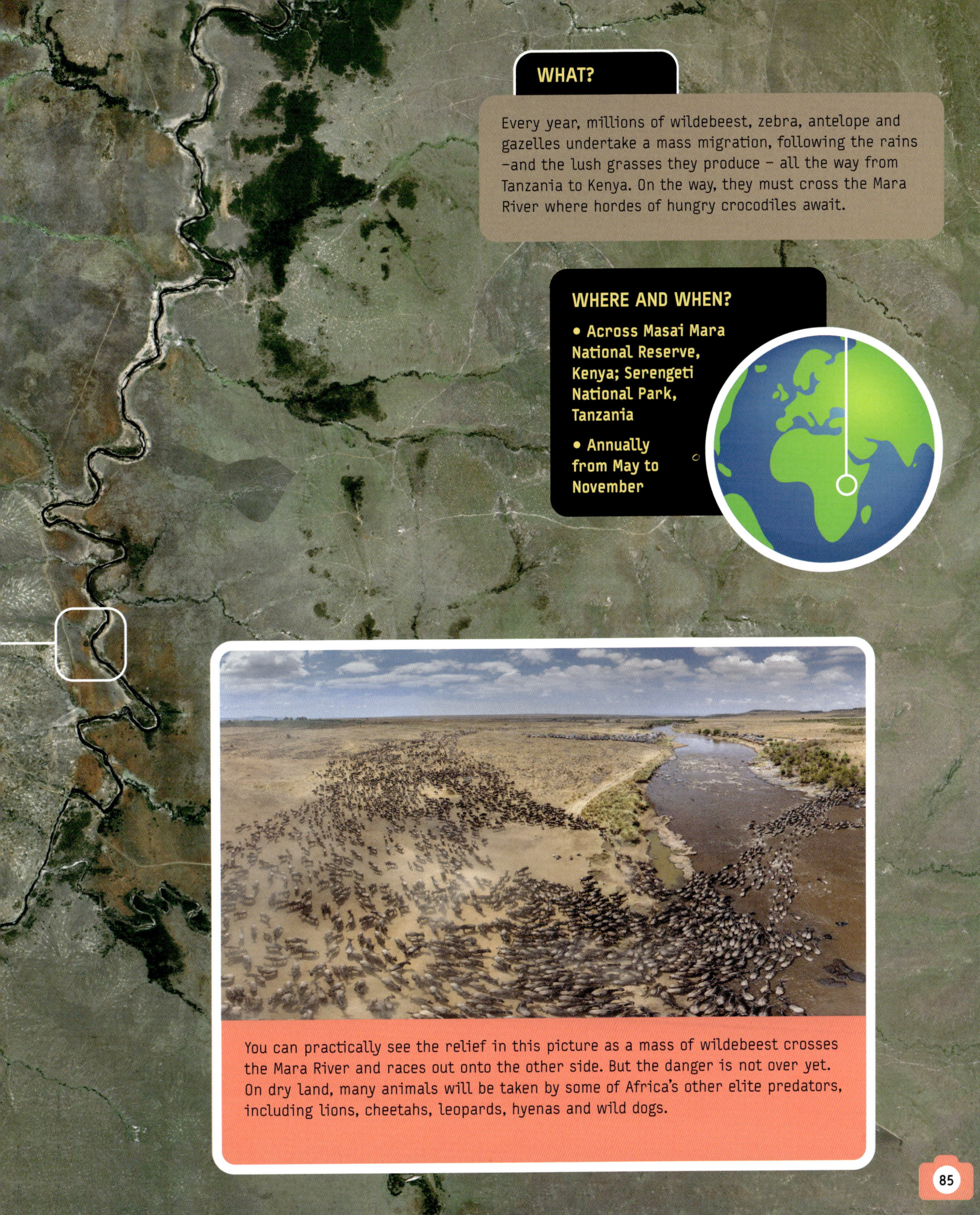

Every year, millions of wildebeest, zebra, antelope and gazelles undertake a mass migration, following the rains –and the lush grasses they produce – all the way from Tanzania to Kenya. On the way, they must cross the Mara River where hordes of hungry crocodiles await.

WHERE AND WHEN?

- **Across Masai Mara National Reserve, Kenya; Serengeti National Park, Tanzania**

- **Annually from May to November**

You can practically see the relief in this picture as a mass of wildebeest crosses the Mara River and races out onto the other side. But the danger is not over yet. On dry land, many animals will be taken by some of Africa's other elite predators, including lions, cheetahs, leopards, hyenas and wild dogs.

VICTORIA FALLS
ZAMBIA–ZIMBABWE

In this aerial image, the Zambezi River cascades over the edge of a 1,680-m (5,500-ft) wide plateau to create one of the world's most spectacular sights: Victoria Falls. Water from the falls plunges 108 m (354 ft) into a gorge below and generates a mist that can be seen for miles around. This gives Victoria Falls its local name, *Mosi-oa-Tunya*, or 'The Smoke that Thunders'.

WHERE?

On the Zambezi River between Zimbabwe to the south and Zambia to the north

Spanning the falls second gorge is the 198-m (650-ft) long Victoria Falls Bridge. Built in 1905 to link Zimbabwe with Zambia, it's a working bridge, carrying trains, automobiles and foot passengers, as well as providing spectacular views.

FISH RIVER CANYON
NAMIBIA

WHAT?

This satellite image seems to show what looks like a cracked patch of mud after being baked in the Sun. It is, however, the Fish River Canyon, the largest canyon in Africa, and one of the largest in the world. The canyon is 160 km (100 miles) long and up to 27 km (17 miles) wide and 700 m (2,300 ft) deep in some places.

WHERE?

In Ai-Ais–Richtersveld Transfrontier Park, southern Namibia

The Fish River Canyon is made up of two parts: a shallow upper canyon, where the rocks are harder and less prone to erosion; and a lower canyon, where the rocks are softer and water has been able to gouge out deep channels. The process of carving out the canyon began over 50 million years ago.

By zooming in, a colourful landscape of red, blue, and yellow rocks is revealed. Zoom in even closer and the Fish River itself appears. Here, it's shown with water, but Namibia's longest river can be dry outside of the January to April wet season. One of the continent's most popular hiking trails runs alongside the river.

CLOSE-UP

CAPE TOWN STADIUM

Built near the shore with Table Mountain as a backdrop, the Cape Town Stadium is a sports arena with a capacity of 58,300 people. Football, rugby union and tennis have all been played in the stadium. It was completed in 2010 as one of the venues to host the Men's FIFA Football World Cup, which was held in South Africa that year.

LION'S HEAD

At 669 m (2,195 ft), Lion's Head is the highest part of a long rocky outcrop near the coast. The other end was once called 'Lion's Tail' (now Signal Hill) as it was thought the whole outcrop resembled a crouching big cat.

CAPE TOWN
SOUTH AFRICA

WHAT?

This seabird's view of Cape Town shows it to be a coastal city. Buildings sprawl seemingly everywhere, except just inland where a number of peaks, including the flat-topped Table Mountain, dominate the skyline. Along with Bloemfontein and Pretoria, Cape Town is one of South Africa's three capital cities.

WHERE AND WHEN?

- In Western Cape, South Africa
- City founded in 1652

CASTLE OF GOOD HOPE

The five-pointed star shape of Cape Town's oldest building is only visible from above. The fortress was constructed like this in the 17th century so soldiers could protect it from several directions at once.

TABLE MOUNTAIN

A symbol of both Cape Town and South Africa, Table Mountain stands 1,086 m (2,563 ft) tall, and looms over the city. It's named after its flat top, which is around 3 km (2 miles) long, and can be seen from up to 200 km (125 miles) out to sea. From above, the mountain has an almost human shape, like a giant struggling to break free from the ground.

ASIA

Asia is the world's largest continent, taking up over a third of all the land on Earth. In this satellite image, its main landscapes are clearly visible. In the north are white, snowy expanses. In the centre and west are the dark browns of steppe (grasslands), the light browns of desert and the snow-capped peaks of the Himalayas, the world's tallest mountain range. In the south and east, dark patches of green mark extensive tropical forests.

DEAD SEA, JORDAN p.102

MOUNT EVEREST, NEPAL p.104

TAJ MAHAL, INDIA p.106

GANGES DELTA, BANGLADESH–INDIA p.108

PALM JUMEIRAH, DUBAI, UAE

Off the coast of Dubai are a number of artificial islands. These include the Palm Jumeirah, which covers an area of around 5 sq km (3 sq miles) and has been designed to resemble a palm tree.

CUA VAN, HA LONG BAY, VIETNAM

Sat among the many islands and inlets of Ha Long Bay is the floating village of Cua Van. The houses here are built atop floating bamboo platforms and linked together with ropes. The people make their living through fishing and tourism.

MOUNT FUJI, JAPAN

An immense cone of white, Mount Fuji is an active volcano and Japan's highest mountain at 3,776 m (12,388 ft). Luckily, it last erupted in 1707.

GREAT WALL OF CHINA, CHINA p.94

TOKYO, JAPAN p.100

SOLAR PANDAS, DATONG, CHINA

These aren't paintings of pandas. They form part of a power station in China and have been made using thousands of solar panels. Each is several hundred metres long. The entire plant covers an area of 6 sq km (2.3 sq miles) and includes an education centre.

SHILINXIA GLASS PLATFORM, CHINA p.96

TIANMEN MOUNTAIN ROAD, CHINA p.98

CHOCOLATE HILLS, PHILIPPINES p.110

MOUNT BROMO, INDONESIA p.112

GREAT WALL OF CHINA
CHINA

Winding its way along some high peaks, the Great Wall is made up not of one, but numerous walls. Building first began in the 7th century BCE, with some sections having been linked by the 3rd century BCE. Most of what you see today was constructed during the Ming Dynasty (1368–1644 CE).

Fortified watchtowers were built at regular intervals along the Great Wall for extra defence. Each watchtower has arrow slits from which missiles could be fired, and was equipped with flags, lanterns and smoke-signals to communicate with the other towers.

WHAT?

One of the world's most famous sites, the Great Wall of China was constructed over several centuries to protect imperial land from northern invaders. At over 21,00 km (13,00 miles) long, it's still the longest human-made structure ever built, and is today a symbol of China.

WHERE?

Across northern China from Hebai Province in the east to Gansu Province in the west

CLOSE-UP

In this close-up view, we can see just a few of the roughly 10 million people who visit the wall every year. The longest and best-preserved section of the Great Wall is around 8,850 km (5,500 miles) long, though not all of it is open to the public. At Badaling, just outside Beijing, it's possible to walk along a 11-km (7-mile) section of the wall.

SHILINXIA GLASS PLATFORM
BEIJING, CHINA

CLOSE-UP

Jutting out 30 m (100 ft) from the cliff, the platform appears to be suspended in the air for those brave enough to step (or lie) on it. Though the structure is built to take the weight of 1,900 people, only 200 are allowed on at any one time.

WHAT?

Looking like a flying saucer or an oversized egg cup, this glass sightseeing platform gives visitors eye-popping views of the Shilinxia Scenic Area, a 12-km (7.5-mile) long gorge. The platform hangs from the side of a cliff, 400 m (1,312 ft) above the gorge's floor, and 800 m (2,624 ft) above sea level.

WHERE AND WHEN?

• Within the Shilinxia Scenic Area, Diaowo Village, Pinggu District, Beijing, China

• Platform opened in 2016

TIANMEN MOUNTAIN ROAD
CHINA

WHAT?

In the main image, we're gazing down from on high on one of the windiest roads ever constructed. Paved with concrete, the 11-km (7-mile) long route makes an astonishing 99 sharp turns as it wiggles its way up the mountain. It gradually ascends from a height of around 200 m (650 ft) to 1,300 m (4,250 ft) above sea level. On the right, a close-up image of a section of the road shows just how often it doubles back on itself.

HEAVEN'S DOOR

Heaven's Door is a large natural archway that sits at the very top of Tianmen Mountain. Visitors can take a 7,455-m (24,459-ft) long cable car ride some of the way to the arch, but then must climb a further 999 steps to walk through it, as the people in this image are doing.

WHERE AND WHEN?

• In Tianmen Mountain National Park, Zhangjiajie, Hunan Province, China

• Road constructed from 1998–2004

SHIBUYA CROSSING

This bird's-eye view of Shibuya Crossing is a classic image of Tokyo, often seen in movies and on TV. It's the busiest pedestrian crossing in the world. At peak times, as many as 3,000 people can be seen walking across the intersection at each green light, which occurs every two minutes. Built in 1932, the crossing is located just outside the busy Shibuya rail station.

YURIKAMOME

This is the western edge of Rainbow Bridge which links Tokyo's mainland with the artificial island of Odaiba. To access the bridge, the automated trains of the Yurikamome transit system ride around a 270-degree loop out over the water.

TOKYO
JAPAN

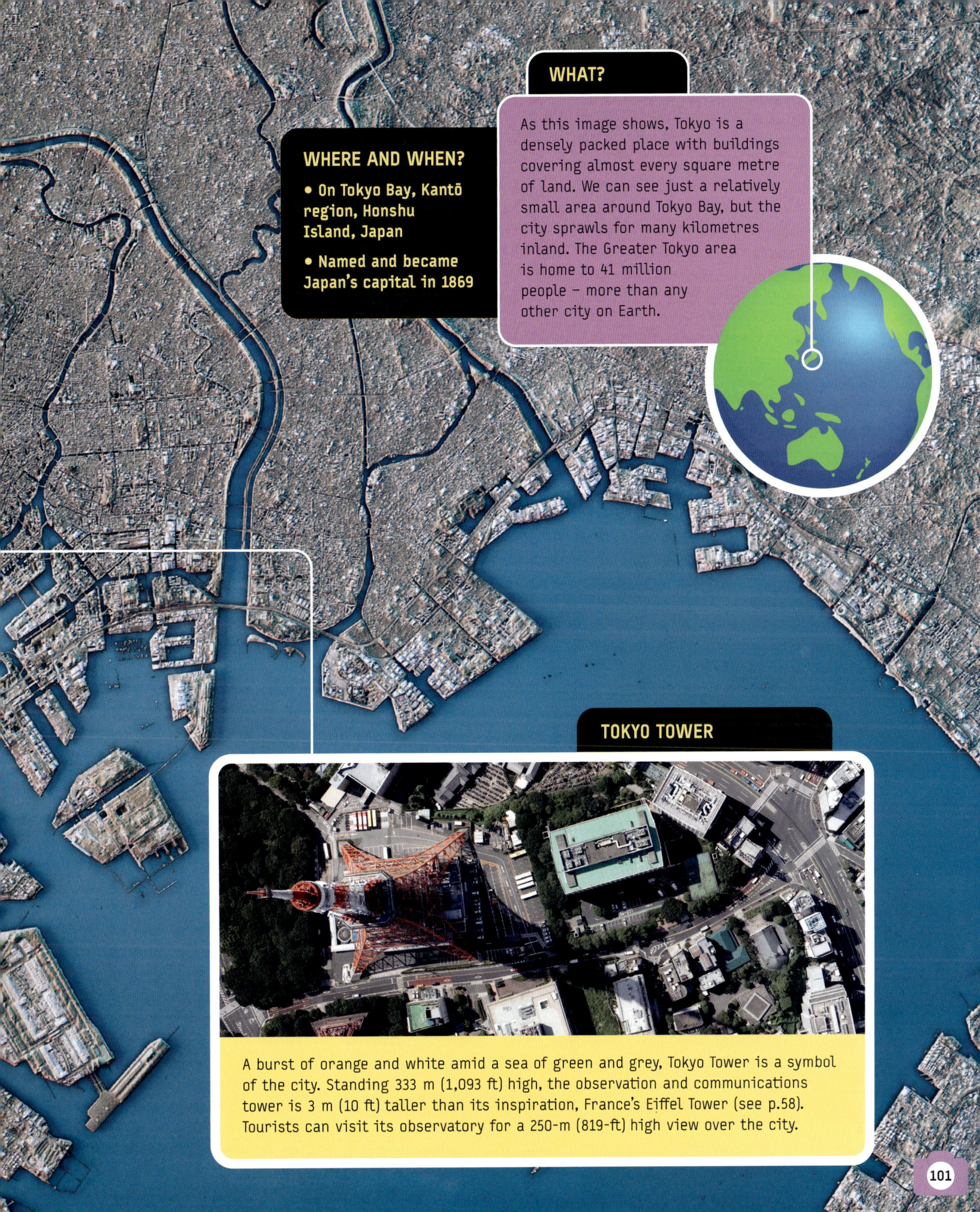

As this image shows, Tokyo is a densely packed place with buildings covering almost every square metre of land. We can see just a relatively small area around Tokyo Bay, but the city sprawls for many kilometres inland. The Greater Tokyo area is home to 41 million people – more than any other city on Earth.

WHERE AND WHEN?

• On Tokyo Bay, Kantō region, Honshu Island, Japan

• Named and became Japan's capital in 1869

TOKYO TOWER

A burst of orange and white amid a sea of green and grey, Tokyo Tower is a symbol of the city. Standing 333 m (1,093 ft) high, the observation and communications tower is 3 m (10 ft) taller than its inspiration, France's Eiffel Tower (see p.58). Tourists can visit its observatory for a 250-m (819-ft) high view over the city.

DEAD SEA
JORDAN

WHAT?

This satellite view shows the Dead Sea as a small blue speck in the centre of the largely brown, arid Middle East. The sea is a landlocked salt lake, located around 430 m (1,410 ft) below sea level, making it not just the lowest body of water on land, but also the very lowest place on land on Earth.

WHERE?

Between Israel and the Palestinian Territories, and Jordan

WHEN?

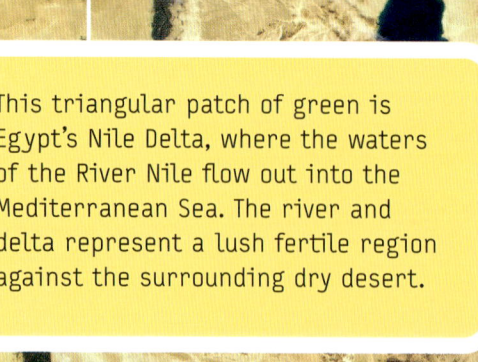

Seen here in close-up, Jordan's salt-evaporation ponds were first constructed in the 1920s. Each pond is separated by 40-m (130-ft) deep walls. The minerals that are harvested here are used to make used to make table salt, road de-icing mixtures and plastics, such as polyvinyl chloride (PVC).

This triangular patch of green is Egypt's Nile Delta, where the waters of the River Nile flow out into the Mediterranean Sea. The river and delta represent a lush fertile region against the surrounding dry desert.

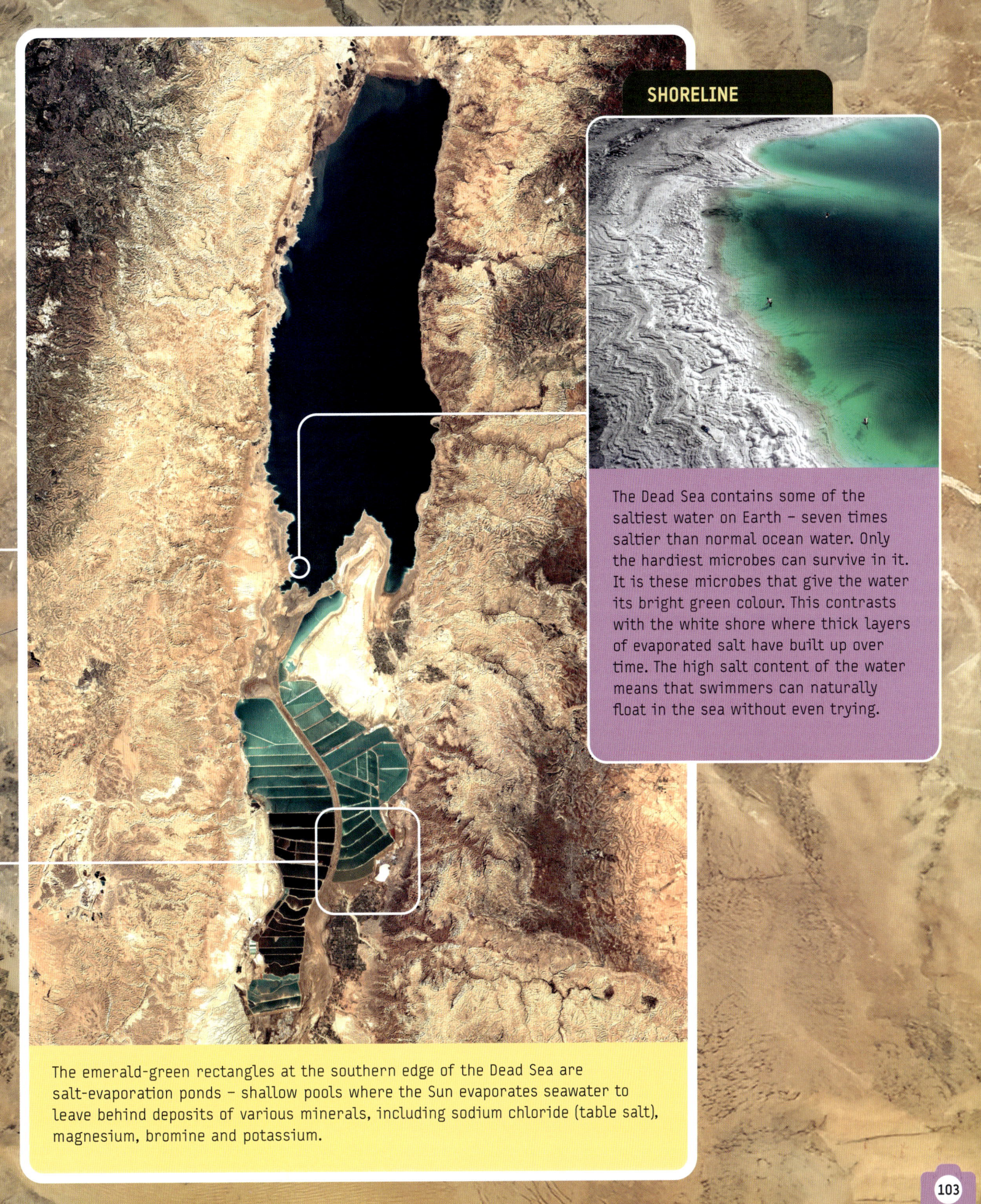

The Dead Sea contains some of the saltiest water on Earth – seven times saltier than normal ocean water. Only the hardiest microbes can survive in it. It is these microbes that give the water its bright green colour. This contrasts with the white shore where thick layers of evaporated salt have built up over time. The high salt content of the water means that swimmers can naturally float in the sea without even trying.

The emerald-green rectangles at the southern edge of the Dead Sea are salt-evaporation ponds – shallow pools where the Sun evaporates seawater to leave behind deposits of various minerals, including sodium chloride (table salt), magnesium, bromine and potassium.

MOUNT EVEREST
NEPAL–CHINA

WHAT?

From the side, the world's tallest mountain dominates the sky, soaring to 8,850 m (29,035 ft) above sea level. But from above (left), you can see how it's just one peak of many in the great Himalayan range that stretches for 2,500 km (1,550 miles) across Central Asia.

WHERE?

In the Himalayan mountain range, on the border between Nepal and China

CLOSE-UP

From far above, the tents of Nepal's South Base Camp resemble yellow sweets dropped in the snow. The camp is the starting point for climbers daring to risk an ascent of Everest. First conquered by New Zealander Edmund Hillary and Tibetan Tenzing Norgay in 1953, Everest has been climbed by over 7,000 people since, and is considered a rite of passage by many mountaineers.

TAJ MAHAL
AGRA, INDIA

WHAT?

WHERE AND WHEN?

- In Agra, Uttar Pradesh, northern India

- Completed in 1648 CE

The main image shows how the Taj Mahal lies just outside the city of Agra on the banks of the Yamuna River. The image above, taken from closer in and from a lower angle, shows it in all its glory. It was built around 400 years ago by the emperor Shah Jahan in memory of his deceased wife, Mumtaz Mahal. It is considered one of the most beautiful buildings ever constructed.

Zooming in even closer, we can see the elaborate tiling that surrounds the central building. The stars are made of brownish-red sandstone, while the diamond-shaped pieces are white marble. The walls of the mausoleum are decorated with semi-precious stones.

By looking straight down on the Taj Mahal, we can see its symmetrical layout. At the centre is a square building, topped with five domes, including a large onion-shaped one in the centre. The tombs of Shah Jahan and Mumtaz Mahal sit below this. A minaret stands on each corner of the building. To the left and right of the main building are two near identical structures. The one on the left is a mosque while the one on the right is a guesthouse.

GANGES DELTA
BANGLADESH–INDIA

SUNDARBANS

The dark green areas in the main image are the Sundarbans, a vast swamp forest. It's made up mainly of mangroves – dense masses of trees with stilt-like roots. They can survive in extremely salty coastal water that would damage most other trees. Further inland, the light green area represents a forest of larger tropical trees plus areas of agricultural land. Boats are the main way of exploring this sodden landscape.

WHAT?

Here, we're looking down at the world's largest river delta, covering an area of over 100,000 sq km (40,000 sq miles). Several rivers, including the mighty Ganges, empty into the ocean here, dividing into hundreds of snake-like waterways as they wind their way to the coast. The rivers deliver vast quantities of sediment – shown here in light blue – into the dark blue sea beyond, as well as fertile soils onto the surrounding floodplain.

WHERE?

On the border of Bangladesh and the Indian state of West Bengal

The forests and waterways of the Ganges Delta provide cover for some of India's most famous predators. These include pythons and the Bengal tiger, shown here. Unlike most big cats, tigers are skilled swimmers. They slip silently through the water to sneak up on their prey which can include deer, boar and monkeys.

CLOSE-UP

CHOCOLATE HILLS
PHILIPPINES

WHEN?

From the sky, these giant grass-covered bumps look like a mysterious, alien landscape. But the mounds are a natural geological formation. In winter, the hills appear lush and green (left), but in summer, the grass dies off and turns brown, giving them their chocolatey appearance.

WHERE?

On Bohol Island, Bohol Province, the Philippines

The image on the left shows a wider view of the hills. In total, there are over 1,700 of them in an area of 50 sq km (20 sq miles). According to local legends, the hills were either boulders thrown by warring giants, or marked the spots where tears were shed by a giant. Scientists say they're formed of ancient limestone, which was gradually eroded by flowing water into these rounded shapes between 2 and 5 million years ago.

MOUNT BROMO
INDONESIA

WHAT?

From space, Mount Bromo looks small and insignificant. It's not even the largest peak in the Tengger Mountains, a cluster of volcanic cones that were formed by a massive eruption around 45,000 years ago. Though relatively small, it is still one of Indonesia's most active volcanoes.

CLOSE-UP

By zooming in on Mount Bromo's caldera (the collapsed circular hole in a volcano's centre), plumes of smoke can be seen, as well as a small pool of water. Bromo has erupted ash and debris several times in the past 30 years. Despite this – and two fatalities caused by the eruptions – it is still possible to follow a 5.5-km (3.4-mile) trail to the top of the volcano. Hikers should wear a mask to protect against the smoke.

WHERE?

In Bromo Tengger Semeru National Park, on the island of Java, Indonesia

HUTT LAGOON, AUSTRALIA

These candy-coloured ponds are part of a 70-sq-km (30-sq-mile) salt lake in Western Australia. Hutt Lagoon gets its vibrant pinks, reds, oranges and purples from algae in its seawater. Used in cosmetics and food colouring, the algae is farmed in the square, artificial ponds, shown here.

NINGALOO REEF, AUSTRALIA

Ningaloo Reef is a 300-km (186-mile) long ecosystem of coral gardens and a dense mixture of marine life. Visitors to the reef can swim with humpback whales and manta rays, though they may want to avoid some other visitors, such as this huge school of sharks.

DAMPIER CREEK, AUSTRALIA p.120

OCEANIA

Blue is the main colour of Oceania, a region that takes up a vast watery swathe of the southern and central Pacific Ocean and encompasses over 10,000 islands. It's dominated by the continent (and country) of Australia. The brown areas mark the desert that covers much of the country's interior. Greener areas are found on the coast where the majority of the population lives. The lush and mountainous islands of New Zealand can be seen to the east.

MOUNT YASUR, VANUATU

Even from far above, smoke can be seen billowing from Mount Yasur, a near-constantly active volcano on the small island of Vanuatu. It's believed to have been erupting for around 800 years, and has been given the nickname the 'Lighthouse of the Pacific' for its near constant glow,

WAIOTAPU, NEW ZEALAND

The Champagne Pool, shown here, in the geothermal area of Waiotapu, is a hot bubbling green spring surrounded by yellow and orange sulphur deposits.

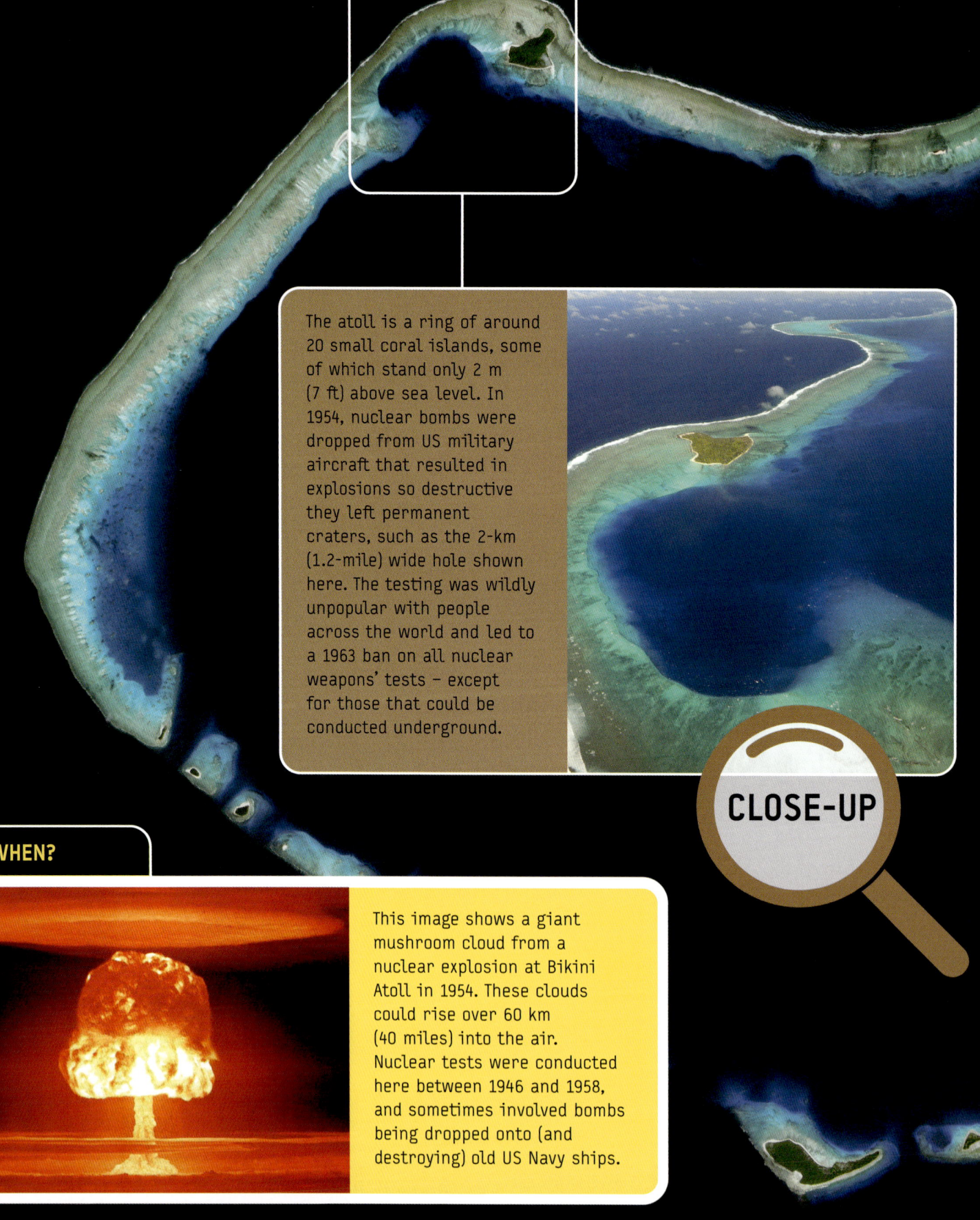

The atoll is a ring of around 20 small coral islands, some of which stand only 2 m (7 ft) above sea level. In 1954, nuclear bombs were dropped from US military aircraft that resulted in explosions so destructive they left permanent craters, such as the 2-km (1.2-mile) wide hole shown here. The testing was wildly unpopular with people across the world and led to a 1963 ban on all nuclear weapons' tests – except for those that could be conducted underground.

CLOSE-UP

This image shows a giant mushroom cloud from a nuclear explosion at Bikini Atoll in 1954. These clouds could rise over 60 km (40 miles) into the air. Nuclear tests were conducted here between 1946 and 1958, and sometimes involved bombs being dropped onto (and destroying) old US Navy ships.

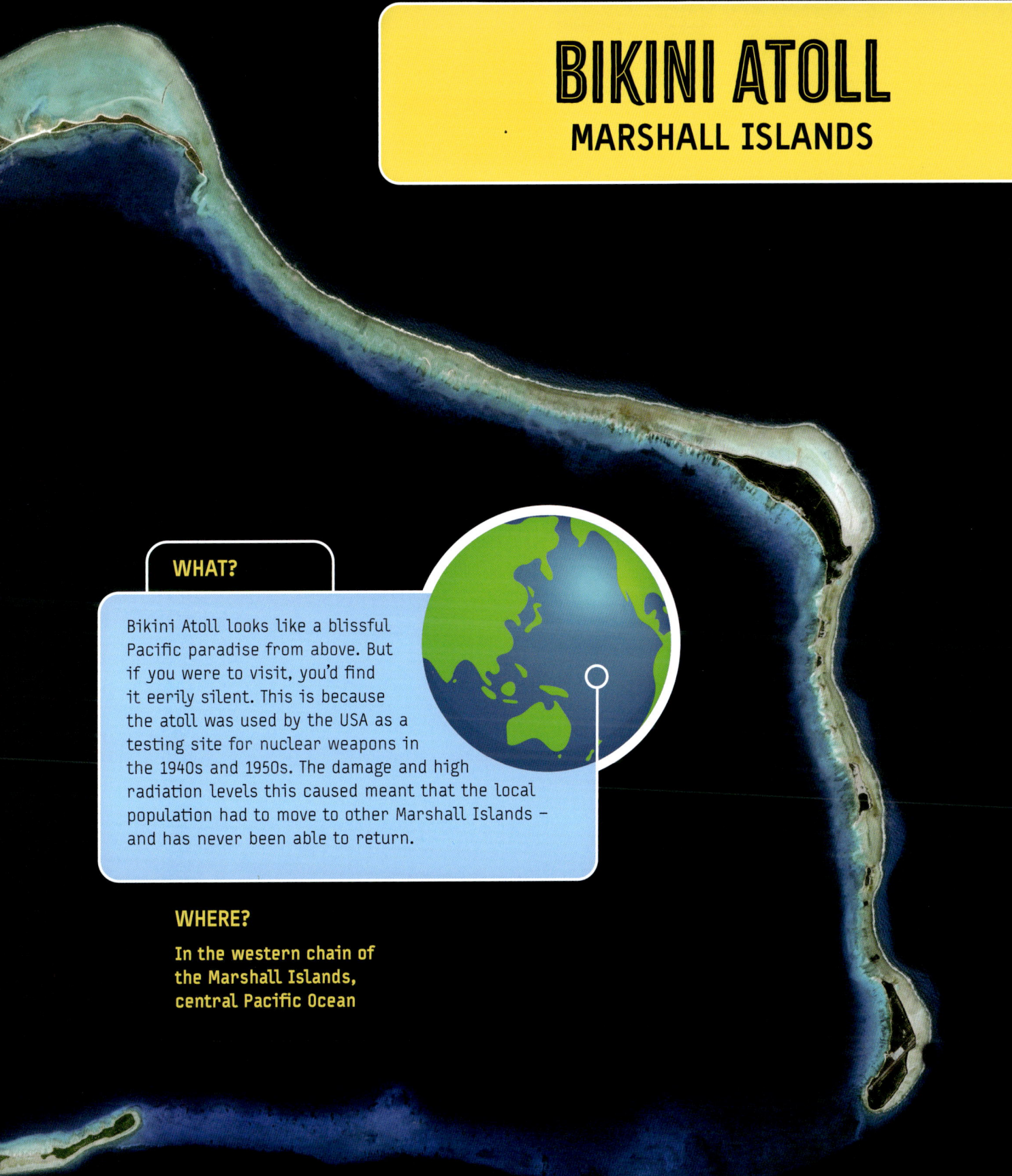

BIKINI ATOLL
MARSHALL ISLANDS

WHAT?

Bikini Atoll looks like a blissful Pacific paradise from above. But if you were to visit, you'd find it eerily silent. This is because the atoll was used by the USA as a testing site for nuclear weapons in the 1940s and 1950s. The damage and high radiation levels this caused meant that the local population had to move to other Marshall Islands – and has never been able to return.

WHERE?

In the western chain of the Marshall Islands, central Pacific Ocean

ROCK ISLANDS
PALAU

CLOSE-UP

The boat in this image gives a good idea of the scale of the Rock Islands. It's shown entering an inlet in Mecherchar Island (also known as Eil Malk), the main island of the group, at roughly 6.5 km (4 miles) long and 4.5 km (3 miles) wide. With ten lakes, an abundance of birdlife, coral reefs and tropical fish, it's the perfect place to take a tourist boat and explore.

WHAT?

Looking like a melted marble from above, the Rock Islands are a unique marine habitat. Hundreds of bright green forested islands can be found clustered together in a lagoon. Erosion has given the islands strange mushroom-like shapes over time. Spread over an area of around 1,000 sq km (385 sq miles), the islands are home to a great variety of plants and wildlife.

WHERE?

In the Southern Lagoon, Koror State, Palau

JELLYFISH LAKE

This isolated lake is home to millions of golden jellyfish. Inside the jellyfish are algae that provide food for the animal. So, every day, the jellyfish migrate across the lake, following the path of the Sun to allow the algae to photosynthesise.

DINOSAUR TRACKS

Just beyond the extent of this picture are more natural wonders: dinosaur tracks. At low tide on some of the nearby beaches, it's possible to see the preserved 130-million-year-old footprints of various dinosaurs. These include stegosaurs and long-necked sauropods.

DAMPIER CREEK
AUSTRALIA

WHAT?

From above, the blue waters of Dampier Creek can be seen winding inland like weird blue tentacles. The creek forms the eastern border of the small coastal town of Broome, which sits on the edge of the Indian Ocean. Broome is a popular tourist destination, and was a centre for pearl diving in the late 19th century.

WHERE?

Just east of the town of Broome, Kimberly region, Western Australia, Australia

CLOSE-UP

Looking more closely, you can see how the creek's meandering tributaries are thick with vegetation. As was the case millions of years ago, the area is rich in wildlife, though today you're more likely to meet turtles, sea snakes, dolphins and a wide variety of birds rather than dinosaurs.

GREAT BARRIER REEF
AUSTRALIA

WHAT?

From above, the world's biggest barrier reef appears as a long string of light blue specks against the darker blue of the ocean. Each speck represents one of more than 2,500 individual coral reefs and 900 islands stretching for over 2,300 km (1,400 miles) and covering 344,400 sq km (133,000 sq miles) of Pacific Ocean. This breathtaking line of beauty is a wildlife hotspot, home to some of the most fascinating creatures on the planet, including whales, turtles, sharks, giant clams and numerous colourful corals.

WHERE?

In the Pacific Ocean off the coast of Queensland, northeastern Australia

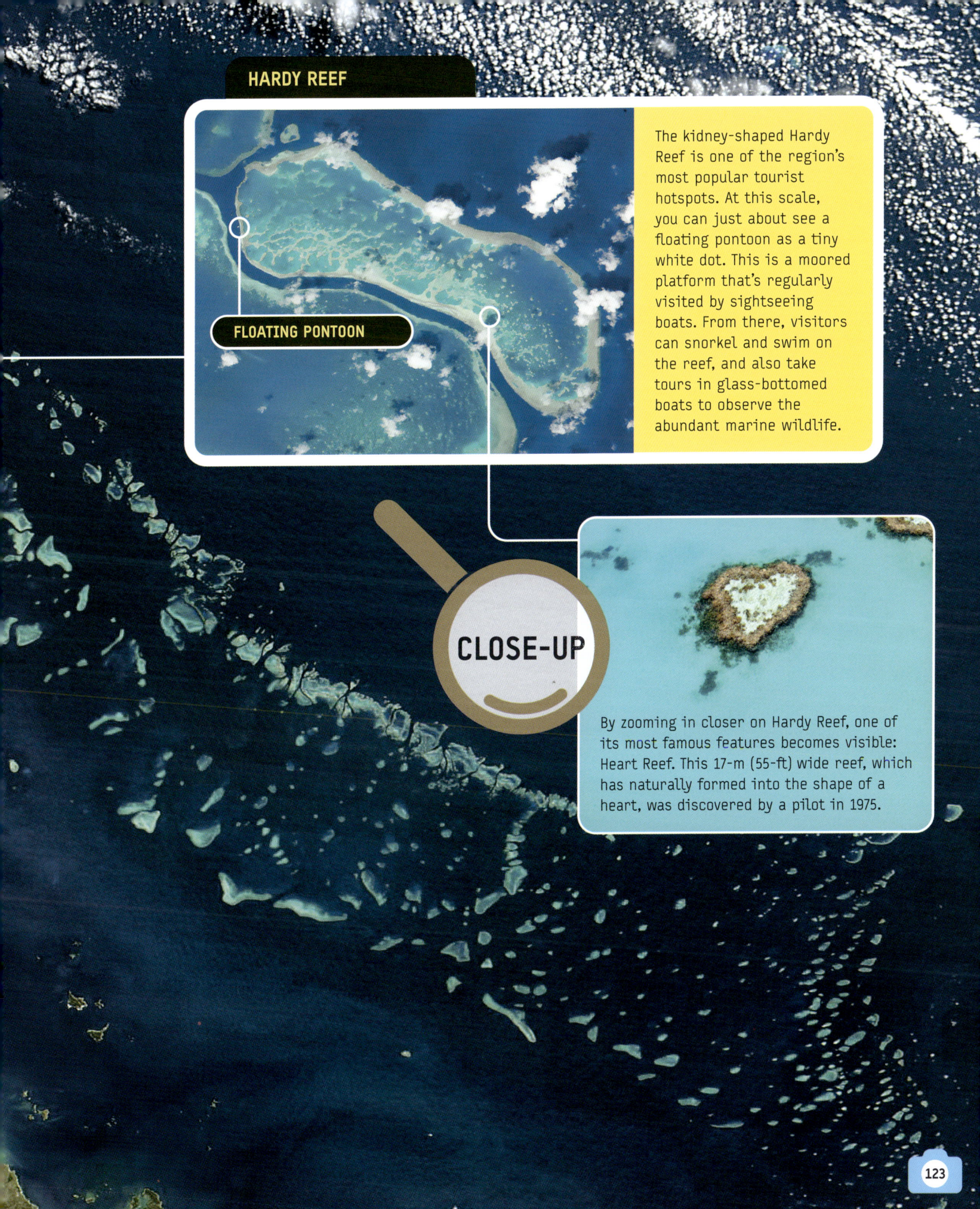

HARDY REEF

FLOATING PONTOON

The kidney-shaped Hardy Reef is one of the region's most popular tourist hotspots. At this scale, you can just about see a floating pontoon as a tiny white dot. This is a moored platform that's regularly visited by sightseeing boats. From there, visitors can snorkel and swim on the reef, and also take tours in glass-bottomed boats to observe the abundant marine wildlife.

CLOSE-UP

By zooming in closer on Hardy Reef, one of its most famous features becomes visible: Heart Reef. This 17-m (55-ft) wide reef, which has naturally formed into the shape of a heart, was discovered by a pilot in 1975.

CLOSE-UP

In this zoomed-in image, we can see two divers entering the water off the *Maryborough*, the first boat to be sunk here (in 1963). To their right is the wreck of the *Platypus II* (sunk 1966), to the left is the *Stingaree* (1966), while straight ahead of them is the *Seal* (1966). Tangalooma's crystal clear waters and mixture of human-made and natural wonders have made it a hugely popular boating, diving and snorkelling site. The name *Tangalooma* means 'where the fish gather' in the language of the local indigenous Quandamooka people.

WHAT?

At first glance, this image appears to show the site of a major disaster. In fact, this epic scene has been created on purpose. Between the 1960s and 1980s, 15 ships were deliberately sunk off the coast of Tangalooma, a resort town in Queensland, Australia. The scuttled ships now provide a home to a great wealth of marine wildlife, including corals, dolphins, turtles and more than 200 species of fish.

WHERE?

On the west side of Moreton Island, Queensland, Australia

TANGALOOMA
AUSTRALIA

CLEAR ISLAND WATERS
GOLD COAST, AUSTRALIA

CLOSE-UP

From this lower-angled view, it is obvious that almost every house in Clear Island Waters has a water view, while several front yards lead down to their own private jetty. Many residents have boats for getting around and providing access to the nearby rivers. The skyscrapers of Gold Coast city can be seen in the distance.

From above, Clear Island Waters looks like a drawing of tentacles in a colouring book or a town made from toy bricks. It is actually a residential suburb built on the artificial Clear Island Lake, Queensland. Around 4,000 people live in the Clear Island Waters community.

WHERE AND WHEN?

• In the city of Gold Coast, Queensland, Australia

• Settlement built in 1990s

THE LAKE IN WET TIMES

The lake consists of Lake Eyre North (shown in this image), which is connected by the narrow Goyder Channel (shown here in green) to Lake Eyre South, which lies outside the frame of this image to the right. Usually one of the driest places on the Australian continent, it is shown here following a rare deluge of rain. As the waters enter the dry lake bed, they mix with sediment and algae to turn parts of Lake Eyre North green and other parts pink.

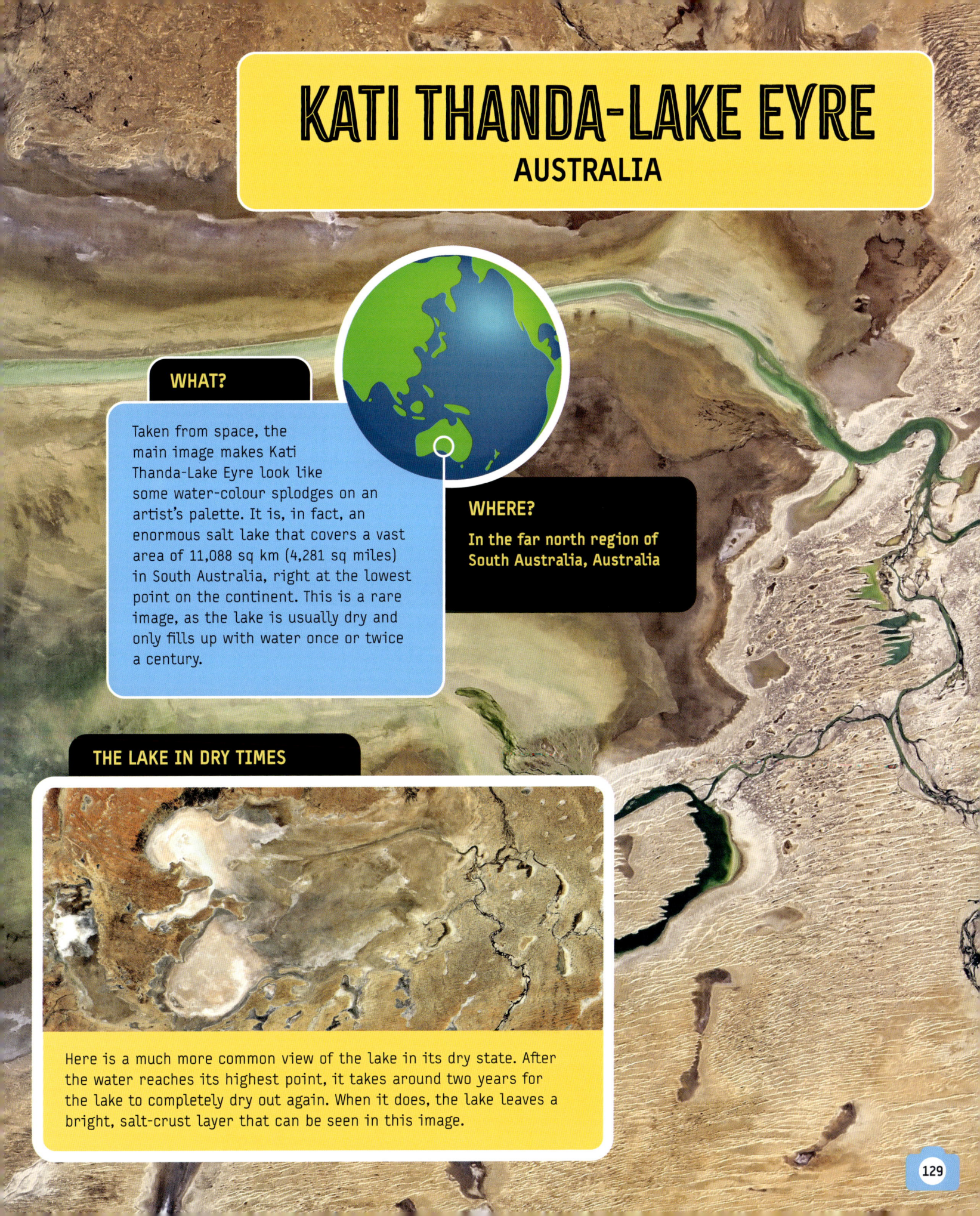

KATI THANDA-LAKE EYRE
AUSTRALIA

WHAT?

Taken from space, the main image makes Kati Thanda-Lake Eyre look like some water-colour splodges on an artist's palette. It is, in fact, an enormous salt lake that covers a vast area of 11,088 sq km (4,281 sq miles) in South Australia, right at the lowest point on the continent. This is a rare image, as the lake is usually dry and only fills up with water once or twice a century.

WHERE?

In the far north region of South Australia, Australia

THE LAKE IN DRY TIMES

Here is a much more common view of the lake in its dry state. After the water reaches its highest point, it takes around two years for the lake to completely dry out again. When it does, the lake leaves a bright, salt-crust layer that can be seen in this image.

SYDNEY
AUSTRALIA

SYDNEY OPERA HOUSE

SYDNEY TOWER

With its gleaming-white roofs shaped like seashells, Sydney Opera House is one of Australia's most recognisable landmarks. Completed in 1973, this multi-purpose venue's main concert hall can seat 2,654 people. There are several smaller theatres, which stage plays, films and concerts.

The tallest structure in the city at 309 m (1,013 ft), the Sydney Tower is a marvel of modern engineering. Opened in 1981, it has been designed to withstand earthquakes – which should be of comfort to the people on its glass-bottomed observation platform and in its two revolving restaurants (which revolve in different directions).

WHAT?

This satellite image shows Australia's largest city in all its glory. Built around a large natural harbour, Sydney sprawls for many kilometres inland. By the water, Sydney Harbour boasts beaches, homes, parks and some of the world's most famous landmarks. On the water, boats whizz backwards and forwards. Residents and tourists alike often get around by water ferry.

WHERE AND WHEN?

- In New South Wales, Pacific Coast, Australia

- City founded in 1788

SYDNEY HARBOUR BRIDGE

Known locally as 'The Coathanger', the 500-m (1,650-ft) long Sydney Harbour Bridge contains railroad tracks, a road and two walkways. It took 2,000 workers eight years to build, opening to the public in 1932.

TE KĀIO BAY

This zoomed-in image shows Te Kāio, also known as Tumbledown Bay. Archaeological evidence, which includes ancient tools, shows that humans once inhabited this area many hundreds of years ago. Today, it's considered to have one of the best beaches in the Christchurch region.

BANKS PENINSULA
NEW ZEALAND

AKAROA HARBOUR

This image shows a lighthouse on Akaroa Harbour, the long inlet linking the sea with the centre of the peninsula – *akaroa* means 'long harbour' in the local language. Māori people have lived in this area for centuries. The first European settlers arrived in the mid-19th century.

WHAT?

Looking like a crumpled piece of colourful aluminium foil from above, Banks Peninsula is one of New Zealand's most unusual landforms. Once an island formed by two volcanic cones, the peninsula was eventually joined to the South Island by sediment from the Waimakariri River. It was named by British explorer Captain Cook in 1770 after his onboard naturalist, Joseph Banks.

WHERE?
Near the city of Christchurch, South Island, New Zealand

ANTARCTICA

CUVERVILLE ISLAND p.136

From above, Antarctica is a vast splash of icy white set against the deep-blue water of the Southern Ocean. The most southerly continent on Earth, Antarctica is also the coldest and driest. Its almost total lack of rain makes Antarctica the world's largest desert, despite its 14.2 million sq km (5.5 million sq miles) being almost completely covered with thick ice. The continent's barren landscape makes it inhospitable to human life, supporting only around 1,000 temporary residents (mainly scientists) at any one time.

LARSEN C ICE SHELF RIFT

This image shows a giant rift, or crack, in an ice shelf. The rift is around 100 m (300 ft) wide, 500 m (1,700 ft) deep and 110 km (70 miles) long and runs along the Larsen C Ice Shelf, a massive slab of Antarctic ice that formed over thousands of years. Scientists first noticed the rift in 2016.

This US research base has been designed to withstand the worst of the Antarctic weather. The horseshoe-shaped modules are connected by flexible tube-corridors, and are set on adjustable columns that can be raised to prevent the station from being buried in snow.

SEA ICE, SOUTHERN OCEAN p.138

MCMURDO DRY VALLEYS

Patches of craggy-brown in amidst the white, McMurdo Dry Valleys are one of the few ice-free areas in Antarctica. They remain dry because the snow is constantly blown away by strong winds.

MCMURDO STATION p.140

CUVERVILLE ISLAND
GRAHAM LAND

WHAT?

From above, Cuverville Island looks like a lump of melted ice cream. However, the white is actually ice and snow that entirely cover the small 2.5-km (1.6-mile) wide island. The brown splodges, meanwhile, are areas of concentrated guano – penguin poo – marking the location of several colonies of gentoo penguins. The island is one of the birds' most important breeding sites.

WHERE?

In the Errera Channel between the Arctowski Peninsula and Ronge Island, off Antarctica's western coast

Below, we can see a penguin colony in close-up. Every year, 6,000 pairs of gentoo penguins visit Cuverville Island to breed. They base their colonies on low-lying beaches near the coast. Pairs of penguins build nests from small rocks lined with feathers. Here, the female will lay two eggs. The parents will then take it in turns both incubating the eggs and, when they're hatched, feeding the chicks.

In this image, one group of penguins is shown heading inland while another pair heads to the sea. The penguins are awkward waddlers on land but, in the water, they are graceful swimmers able to reach speeds of 36 kph (22 mph) – faster than any other diving bird.

CLOSE-UP

SEA ICE
SOUTHERN OCEAN

WHAT?

This striking view could be tiny tile pieces from a mosaic. In fact, it shows thousands of pieces of sea ice off the coast of Antarctica. Sea ice is frozen seawater that forms in the ocean in the winter and melts during the summer, breaking up into blocks. These blocks are known as floes and can be anything from a few metres to hundreds of metres across – such as the ones on the right-hand side of this picture.

WHERE?

Around 65 km (40 miles) off the coast of Antarctica in the Southern Ocean

MCMURDO STATION
ROSS ISLAND

HOW?

In order to support the people living and working at McMurdo, the buildings are heavily insulated. Warmth is now provided by diesel generators – although from 1962 to 1972, the base was heated by a small nuclear power station. There are few comforts here, with scientists sleeping in bunk beds and using portable toilets.

From above, McMurdo Station looks like a science-fiction settlement on another planet. From the ground, it becomes clear that this is a research station. Around 150 buildings make up McMurdo Station, which acts as a headquarters for the US Antarctic Programme, and can house 1,100 people at one time, making it the largest community in Antarctica.

WHERE AND WHEN?

- On Ross Island, Antarctica

- Founded in 1956

ROSS ISLAND

McMurdo Station's location at the southern tip of Ross Island means it is surrounded by sea ice for most of the year. This wider image shows it just as the sea ice is breaking up. In winter, temperatures at the station can drop as low as -50°C (-58°F), and up to 1.5 m (4.9 ft) of snow can fall. When severe weather conditions make reaching the base difficult by air, icebreaker ships are brought in. During winter, when it's dark most of the time, the number of people staying here may be as few as 100.

141

WHAT?

From above, McMurdo Station looks like a science-fiction settlement on another planet. From the ground, it becomes clear that this is a research station. Around 150 buildings make up McMurdo Station, which acts as a headquarters for the US Antarctic Programme, and can house 1,100 people at one time, making it the largest community in Antarctica.

WHERE AND WHEN?

• On Ross Island, Antarctica

• Founded in 1956

ROSS ISLAND

McMurdo Station's location at the southern tip of Ross Island means it is surrounded by sea ice for most of the year. This wider image shows it just as the sea ice is breaking up. In winter, temperatures at the station can drop as low as -50°C (-58°F), and up to 1.5 m (4.9 ft) of snow can fall. When severe weather conditions make reaching the base difficult by air, icebreaker ships are brought in. During winter, when it's dark most of the time, the number of people staying here may be as few as 100.

INDEX

CREDITS

The publisher would like to thank the following for their kind permission to reproduce their images

Key l=left, r=right, t=top, b=bottom, c=center

All rights reserved.

Front Cover: Shutterstock/GaudiLab
Back Cover: c Shutterstock/Npeter tl Shutterstock/Victoria Schaefer, tcl Shutterstock/Gianfranco Vivi, bcl Shutterstock/abriendomundo, bl Shutterstock/ByDroneVideo, tr Shutterstock/ SW arts, tcr Shutterstock/ImAAm, bcr Shutterstock/Abolaji Rasaq br Shutterstock/Mar Pages

Interiors: p1 c Shutterstock/Npeter; pp2-3 NASA, p2 tl Shutterstock/GaudiLab; p3 br NASA; pp4-5 Maxar Technologies; pp6-7 NASA, p6 tl Shutterstock/Victoria Schaefer, p6 tr Thierry Grun - Aero, p6 br Creative Commons/Alexandre Cesar Salem e Silva, p7 t Getty Images/STR; p7 cr Shutterstock/Tanya Puntti, p7 cl Shutterstock/ImAAm, p7 b Maxar Technologies; pp8-9 NASA, p8 tl NASA, p8 tr Maxar Technologies, p9 tr Maxar Technologies, p9 br iStock/ViewApart; pp10-11 Shutterstock/Trphotos, p11 tr Shutterstock/Vadim 777, p11 br Shutterstock/Best-Backgrounds; pp12-13 NASA, p12 tl Shutterstock/Donaldb, p12 bl Shutterstock/Bento Orlando, p13 tl Shutterstock Gorodenkoff, p13 br Alamy/Tetra Images; pp14-15 Shutterstock/Jeffrey Milstein, p15 t Shutterstock/Sergii Figurnyi, p15 b Getty Images/dolphinphoto; pp16-17 Shutterstock/Mak3t; p18 Shutterstock GaudiLab, p19 t Alamy/Aleksandar Tomic, p19 bl Shutterstock/Oscar Chamorro; p19 br Alamy/ istoric Illustrations; pp20-21 Shutterstock/Victoria Schaefer, p20 cl Shutterstock/Lane V. Erickson, p21 tr Shutterstock/NayaDadara, p21 br Shutterstock/es3n; pp22-23 Maxar Technologies, p23 tr Shutterstock/Daniela Constantinescu; pp24-25 Alamy/Universal Images Group North America LLC, p24 tr, p24 bl Shutterstock/Aberu.Go, p24 br Maxar Technologies, p25 br Maxar Technologies; pp26-27 Maxar Technologies, p26 bl Shutterstock/GTW, p27 t Shutterstock/Aleksandr Medvedkov, p27 br Shutterstock Shee Heng Chong; pp28-29 Maxar Technologies, p28 tr Shutterstock/Joe Benning, p28 br Getty Images/Lars Leemann, p29 t Shutterstock/Gianfranco Vivi; pp30-31 NASA, p30 bl Getty Images/Anadolu, p30 tr Shutterstock/John Kershner,

p31 bl Shutterstock/ByDroneVideos, p31 tr Shutterstock/abriendomundo; pp32-33 Science Photo Library/Airpano-Amazing Aerial Agency, p32 bl Shutterstock/Douglas Olivares, p33 t Alamy/Juergen Ritterbach, p33 br Shutterstock/Adwo; pp34-35 NASA, p34 cl Maxar Technologies, p35 t Getty Images/Collart Hervé, p35 br Alamy/Pulsar Imagens, pp36-37 Shutterstock/Alexandree, p37 tr Shutterstock/vitmark, p37 b Shutterstock/Laura Morris; pp38-39 Alamy/ManuelMata, p38 bl Alamy/Claudia Weinmann, p39 t Getty Images/DigitalGlobe, p39 bl Maxar Technologies; pp40-41 NASA, p40 bl Maxar Technologies, p41 tl Shutterstock/victor eleuterio; pp42-p43 Getty Images/Gallo Images, p42 bl Shutterstock/R.M. Nunes, p42 tr Shutterstock/Donatas Dabravolskas, p43 tr Getty Images/Marcelo Nacinovic, p43 br Shutterstock/Marcelo Nacinovic; pp44-45 Creative Commons/Alexandre Cesar Salem e Silva, p44 cr Shutterstock/Iurii Dzivinskyi, p45 t Getty Images/Carl de Souza; pp46-47Alamy/Universal Images Group North America LLC, p46 br Shutterstock/Brester Irina, p47 c Maxar Technologies; pp48-49 USGS/ESA, p49 bl Maxar Technologies; pp50-51 NASA, p50 tr Shutterstock/Alexey Fedorenko (Neuschwanstein shown courtesy of Bayerische Schlösserver-waltung www.schloesser.bayern.de), p50 br Shutterstock/Aerial-motion, p51 tl Shutterstock/SW arts, p51 tr Science Photo Library/Airpano-Amazing Aerial Agency, p51 br Shutterstock/Sadoglu Media; pp52-53 Maxar Technologies, p52 bl Shutterstock/Palmi Gudmundsson, p53 c Shutterstock/iso_phactory, p53 bl Getty Images/Arctic-Images; pp54-55 Maxar Technologies, p54 tl Getty Images/Jason Hawkes, p54 br Shutterstock/GagliardiPhotography, p55 t Shutterstock/Pandora Pictures, p55 br Shutterstock/Skyshark Media; pp56-57 Maxar Technologies, p56 tl Alamy/Roger Cracknell 01-classic, p57 t Shutterstock/High Level, p57 br Shutterstock/marietta peros; pp58-59 Maxar Technologies, p58 cl Shutterstock/StockBrunet, p58 br Shutterstock/Jeffrey Milstein, p59 c Alamy/Tuul and Bruno Morandi, pp60-61 NASA, p60 br Getty Images/Planet Observer, p61 bl Shutterstock/Venturelli Luca, p61 cr AdobeStock/SimonMichael; pp62-63 Alamy/Thierry GRUN - Aero, p62 bl Alamy/Bailey-Cooper Photography, p63 br Shutterstock/Aerial-motion; pp64-65 AdobeStock/Satellite Stocks, p64

bl Shutterstock/Collection Maykova, p65 t Science Photo Library/Alexender Baert-Amazing Aerial Agency, p65 b Shutterstock/Aerial-motion; pp66-67 Shutterstock/Vunav, p67 r Getty Images/Pol Albarrán; pp68-69 Getty Images/DigitalGlobe-ScapeWare3d, p68 br Getty Images/Vasilis Protopapas, p69 br Getty Images/George Pachantouris; pp70-71 NASA, p70 tl Shutterstock/Taghlaouifotos, p70 tr Maxar Technologies, p70 br Shutterstock/Mar Pages, p71 t Maxar Technologies, p71 br Shutterstock/Myroslava Bozhko; p72 Shutterstock/ImAAm, p73 tl Shutterstock/EaglePOV, p73 AdobeStock/Satellite Stocks; pp74-75 Maxar Technologies, p74 br Getty Images/Timothy Allen, p75 tr Alamy/Tony Eveling, p75 bl Shutterstock/Watch The World; pp76-77 Getty Images/Ignacio Palacios, p77 t Shutterstock/Lukas Bischoff Photograph, p77 b Maxar Technologies; p78 Maxar Technologies, p79 Getty Images/Eric Lafforgue-Art in All of Us; pp80-81 Maxar Technologies, p80 cl Getty Images/Planet Observer, p81 bl NASA; pp82-83 Shutterstock/Abolaji Rasaq, p82 b Shutterstock/Tayvay, p83 r Shutterstock/Tolu Owoeye; pp84-85 Shutterstock/Hyserb, p84 cl AWL Images/Paul Joynson Hicks, p84 br Getty Images/Martin Harvey, p85 b Science Photo Library/Airpano-Amazing Aerial Agency; pp86-87 Shutterstock/Vadim Petrakov, p87 br Shutterstock/Adwo; p88 Science Photo Library/US Geological Survey, p89 Maxar Technologies, p89 b Alamy/AfriPics.com; pp90-91 Alamy/Universal Images Group North America LLC, p90 tl Shutterstock/Grant Duncan-Smith, p90 bl Shutterstock/Daniel Harwardt, p91 tl Getty Images/Hoberman Collection, p91 b Shutterstock/Jean van der Meulen; pp92-93 NASA, p92 bl Getty Images/NurPhoto, p92 br Shutterstock/Nguyen Quang Ngoc Tonkin, p93 t Getty Images/ppengcreative, p93 cr Maxar Technologies; pp94-95 Shutterstock/Michael Linde, p94 bl Science Photo Library/Airpano-Amazing Aerial Agency, p94 tr Alamy/RubberBall, p95 b Alamy/Imago; pp96-97 Getty Images/STR-AFP; pp98-99 Maxar Technologies, p98 br Shutterstock/Thongchai.s, p99 cr Shutterstock/Thanachet Maviang; pp100-101 Getty Images/FrankRamspott, p100 tl Shutterstock/Sean Pavone, p100 bl Shutterstock/Fly_and_Dive, p101 b Getty Images/flashfilm; pp102-103 Shutterstock/Best-Backgrounds, p102 br Shutterstock/lavizzara, p103 c Shutterstock/lavizzara, p103 tr Getty Images/Anadolu;

p104 NASA, p104 br Getty Images/AFP, p105 Shutterstock/Arsgera; pp106-107 Science Photo Library/Airbus Defence and Space, p106 bl Shutterstock/Uladzik Kryhin, p107 tr Shutterstock/Sam DCruz, p107 b Shutterstock/Uladzik Kryhin; pp108-109 Shutterstock/Best-Backgrounds, p108 tl Shutterstock/Sk Hasan Ali, p109 br Getty Images/Abstract Aerial Art; pp110-111 Getty Images/Cavan Images-Per-Andre Hoffmann, p110 br Maxar Technologies, p111 t Shutterstock/Oscar Espinosa; p112 Science Photo Library/Planetobserver, p112 br Maxar Technologies, p113 Getty Images/NurIsmailPhotography; pp114-115 NASA, p114 tl Shutterstock/Agent Wolf, p114 tr Shutterstock/Lewis Burnett, p115 tr Maxar Technologies, p115 br Shutterstock/donvictorio; p116-117 Maxar Technologies, p116 cr Getty Images/The Asahi Shimbun, p116 bl United States Department of Energy; pp118-119 Maxar Technologies, p118 bl Shutterstock/Romaine W, p119 bl Shutterstock/Ethan Daniels, p119 br Shutterstock/dvlcom; pp120-121 Maxar Technologies, p120 tl Shutterstock/chrisontour84, p121 b Shutterstock/Aerometrex; pp122-123 NASA, p123 t NASA, p123 cr Shutterstock/Tanya Puntti; pp124-125 Shutterstock/Coral Brunner, p124 t Shutterstock/Drone Chicks; pp126-127 Maxar Technologies, p126 b Alamy/Addictive Stock Creatives; pp128-129 Shutterstock/Best-Backgrounds, p129 bl Maxar Technologies; pp130-131 Maxar Technologies, p130 cl Shutterstock/Vibe Images, p130 cr Shutterstock/Jamen Percy, p131 br Shutterstock/Jamen Percy; pp132-133 Maxar Technologies, p132 cl Shutterstock/Jakub Maculewicz, p133 t Shutterstock/michael schollum; pp134-135 NASA, p134 b Science Photo Library/British Antarctic Survey, p135 tr Science Photo Library/National Science Foundation, p135 br Getty Images/Universal History Archive; pp136-137 Maxar Technologies, p137 t Alamy/Wolfgang Kaehler, p137 br Alamy/Tasfoto; pp138-139 Maxar Technologies; pp140-141 Getty Images/DigitalGlobe-ScapeWare3d, p140 b Shutterstock/james_stone76, p141 b Getty Images/Gallo Images; pp142-143 NASA; p144 NASA